# THE INTERCITY ELECTRIC RAILWAY INDUSTRY IN CANADA

# CANADIAN STUDIES IN ECONOMICS

A series of studies, formerly edited by V. W. Bladen and now edited by Wm. C. Hood, sponsored by the Social Science Research Council of Canada, and published with financial assistance from the Canada Council

# THE INTERCITY

# ELECTRIC RAILWAY INDUSTRY

# IN CANADA

## John F. Due
*University of Illinois*

UNIVERSITY OF TORONTO PRESS

# PREFACE

THIS VOLUME is in a sense a companion piece to the author's study (undertaken jointly with Professor George Hilton of Stanford University) of the electric interurban railway industry in the United States (*The Electric Interurban Railways in America*, Stanford, 1960). Although the United States study contained some reference to Canadian lines, this was incidental to the main purpose of the volume, and there appeared to be sufficient material on the Canadian roads, and sufficient differences from the United States experience, to make a separate study worth while. Fortunately, in the early fifties I had visited the lines then still in operation in Canada, and thus had enjoyed at least a limited personal contact with them.

The author would like to express his appreciation for the assistance provided by a number of individuals and business firms in Canada. These include Mr. Philip T. Clark, comptroller of revenue in Ontario, now retired; Mr. Hugh Brown, FCA, deputy provincial treasurer of Ontario; Canadian National Railways, and particularly Mr. J. A. McDonald; Canadian Pacific Railways; Ontario Northland Railway; British Columbia Electric Railway; Greater Winnipeg Transit Commission; Dominion Bureau of Statistics.

I am also greatly indebted to the three persons who read the original manuscript, Professor J. J. Talman, Professor A. W. Currie, and Mr. John M. Mills, for their suggestions for improvement and their discovery of errors.

Appreciation is also expressed to the Upper Canada Railway Society, and particularly to Mr. E. A. Jordan, for their assistance in compiling photographs of electric railway equipment; to the individuals who provided copies of the photographs used; and to the Stanford University Press, to McGraw-Hill, Inc., and to Southam-Maclean Publications Limited for permission to reproduce various maps which originally appeared in their publications.

The Graduate Research Board of the University of Illinois provided funds for statistical work and typing.

This work has been published with the help of a grant from the Social Science Research Council of Canada, using funds provided by the Canada Council.

*Urbana, Illinois*                                                                    J.F.D.
*July 1, 1965*

# CONTENTS

# LIST OF ILLUSTRATIONS

PLATES (*between pages* 22 *and* 23)

Hamilton Radial Railway no. 305

British Columbia Electric Railway no. 1301

London and Port Stanley Railway heavy steel car

Grand River Railway no. 844

Niagara, St. Catharines and Toronto Railway no. 83

Quebec Railway, Light and Power Company no. 452

Windsor, Essex and Lake Shore Railway no. 505

Canadian National Railways no. 17

## MAPS AND GRAPHS

# INTRODUCTION

THE COMPLETION of the evening run from Port Colborne to Thorold, Ontario, by cars no. 620 and no. 623 of the Niagara, St. Catharines and Toronto Railway on Saturday, March 29, 1959, marked the end of the intercity electric railway industry in Canada. Although some of the trackage remains in freight service, the discontinuance of scheduled passenger service brought the end of the industry as such, because the feature which distinguished it from the railroad was the electric passenger car. The trackage still in freight service became merely an element in the general railroad network. By a strange quirk of history the first run of an electric car in intercity service in Canada also was made to Thorold, in this instance from St. Catharines over the seven-mile line of the St. Catharines, Merritton and Thorold Electric Street Railway, seventy-two years before on October 5, 1887.

In the intervening period, twenty-five companies operated in the industry, with a total of 856 miles of line and an investment of roughly $32 million. It was never a major industry, but its role in the transition of Canadian land transportation from almost sole reliance on the steam railroad to dominance of the motor vehicle should not be overlooked. Far more information is available on the firms than is typical of other industries, primarily because the former were subject to regulation and therefore statistics of their operation were consistently collected.

The electric railway lines never reached the status of an integrated network in Canada as they did in the midwestern United States where virtually every city and town of any size was served by an electric line, and relatively long distance travel—up to 200 miles or more—was not uncommon. Although much of Canada was clearly unsuited to this form of transport because of the light population density, it is somewhat surprising that western and south-central Ontario, parts of Quebec, and even portions of the Maritime provinces did not have more lines, because they had many features in common with the area of the United States south of the Great Lakes. The explanation lies partly in the fact that the development came later in Canada—even though some of the earliest lines in North America were Canadian—so that further growth was cut off by the coming of the motor vehicle before the network of lines was complete. The mileage of lines for which charters were obtained but which were never built exceeded the mileage actually completed.

A note on terminology is necessary. The words "intercity electric railway" as used in this study refer to an intercity electrically operated rail line providing passenger service with cars containing motors. Electrified segments of main line railroads, such as the Montreal suburban service, or purely suburban street car routes, such as the Lachine line of Montreal Tramways, are not included. In the United States, the term "interurban" was universally used for electric intercity lines in the areas in which they were most common—the midwest and Pacific coast states. But this word was rarely employed in Canada, except to some extent in British Columbia. Only one line carried the word in its corporate title, namely, the Edmonton Interurban, a non-electrified short line in Alberta. The Canadian lines were simply referred to as electric railways, and, in Ontario, as radials. Even three city street car systems, those of Guelph, Edmonton, and Peterborough, had the word "radial" in their corporate titles, though they never extended beyond the city areas. This was an appropriate term, because the lines typically extended outward from cities, but it was never used in the United States in this sense, except at a later date in reference to truck lines operating in several directions outward from a large city.

No general history of the industry in Canada has ever been written, and there is only the briefest reference to it in general histories of transportation or of particular major rail systems. The first part of this monograph presents a general review of the development, characteristics, financial situation, and decline of the industry, and the second part provides a brief history of each of the twenty-five companies. These histories have been based primarily on the accounts of the companies over the years in the journal, *Canadian Railway and Marine World*, now *Canadian Transportation*. This source has been supplemented by references in regional histories, contemporary newspapers, articles in various journals and magazines, reports of regulatory bodies, and information supplied by the companies themselves, including firms which were parents of now-abandoned lines, and successors to the original companies. Financial data have been obtained primarily from the series on electric railways originally compiled by the Department of Railways and Canals, and in later years by the Dominion Bureau of Statistics. Every effort has been made to check information from more than one source, but for some of the lines information is so limited that verification has been difficult, and some errors may not have been uncovered.

PART I

THE INDUSTRY

# ABBREVIATIONS

Abbreviations are given only for the Canadian lines which actually operated, plus the Toronto Eastern, and only for the names which the companies used for a substantial period.

## ELECTRIC RAILWAYS

| | |
|---|---|
| BCE | British Columbia Electric Ry. Co. |
| B&H | Brantford and Hamilton Electric Ry. Co. |
| CBE | Cape Breton Electric Co. |
| CBT | Cape Breton Tramways, Ltd. (later S&GB) |
| CW&LE | Chatham, Wallaceburg and Lake Erie Ry. Co. |
| GR | Grand River Ry. Co. |
| GV | Grand Valley Ry. Co. |
| HE | Hull Electric Co. |
| HG&B | Hamilton, Grimsby and Beamsville Electric Ry. Co. |
| HR | Hamilton Radial Electric Ry. Co. |
| H&D | Hamilton and Dundas Street Ry. Co. |
| L&LE | London and Lake Erie Ry. and Transportation Co. (formerly SWT) |
| L&PS | London and Port Stanley Ry. Co. |
| LE&N | Lake Erie and Northern Ry. Co. |
| M&SC | Montreal and Southern Counties Ry. Co. |
| NC | Nipissing Central Ry. Co. |
| NFP&R | Niagara Falls Park and River Ry. Co. |
| NStC&T | Niagara, St. Catharines and Toronto Ry. Co. |
| PC | Pictou County Electric Co. (Egerton Tramways) |
| QRL&P | Quebec Ry., Light and Power Co. |
| S&GB | Sydney and Glace Bay Ry. Co. (formerly CBT) |
| SWT | South Western Traction Co. (became L&LE) |
| SW&A | Sandwich, Windsor and Amherstburg Ry. Co. |
| TE | Toronto Eastern Ry. Co. |
| TS | Toronto Suburban Ry. Co. |
| T&YR | Toronto and York Radial Ry. Co. |
| WE&LS | Windsor, Essex and Lake Shore Rapid Ry. Co. (later Windsor, Essex and Lake Shore Electric Ry. Association) |
| WS&LW | Winnipeg, Selkirk and Lake Winnipeg Ry. Co. |
| WTV&I | Woodstock, Thames Valley and Ingersoll Electric Ry. Co. |

## OTHER RAILWAYS

| | |
|---|---|
| CNR | Canadian National Ry. Co. |
| CPR | Canadian Pacific Ry. Co. |
| TTC | Toronto Transportation Commission |

## CHAPTER ONE

# DEVELOPMENT

THE GRADUAL DEVELOPMENT of knowledge of the nature and capabilities of electric power during the nineteenth century inevitably led to experiments in various countries with the use of this power for purposes of transportation. As early as 1834 a battery-powered motor operated a small car on a short section of track in Vermont, and by 1851 a car of this type made an experimental run from Washington to Bladensburg, Maryland. Progress was slow, and not until the development in the 1870's of the principle of producing electric power by means of a dynamo, thus freeing electric traction from a battery, were real advances possible. It was a German, Werner von Siemens, who produced the first successful electric locomotive in 1879 and exhibited it at the Berlin Industrial Exhibition in that year. Two years later he built the first commercial line, at Lichterfelte, in the suburbs of Berlin.

Meanwhile, in the United States and Canada experiments became more widespread. Thomas Edison designed an experimental locomotive in 1880. In 1884–85 several short commercial passenger lines in Cleveland and elsewhere were built, but not operated successfully for any length of time. The most promising of these was a three-mile line in Baltimore, built by a photographer named Leo Daft, who had taken over the management of a small electric power plant. The third-rail power source employed was not successful, and Daft shifted to a two-overhead-wire system, with a small "troller" running along on the wires; from this came the word "trolley."

The other major developer of electric traction in the mid-eighties was Charles J. Van Depoele, a Belgian who had experimented with the electric operation of cars as a side line to his furniture manufacturing business in Chicago. In 1884 he completed an arrangement with the Exhibition Association of Toronto, which managed the annual Toronto Agricultural Fair, for the operation of an electric passenger railway to the main section of the fair grounds from the Strachan Avenue entrance, where the city horse-car lines ended. A generating plant was set up on the fair grounds, and rails laid. Power was transmitted through a copper strip set in a box between the rails. A motor car towed three small open passenger cars, which were built locally for the lines. During the ten days of the operation of the fair in August, the little train carried thousands of passengers who marvelled at the invention. In some respects this was the first successful operation of an electric passenger-carrying road in North America. The Toronto papers commented at length on the success of the line.

The conduit power source had given difficulties, however, and the following summer was replaced by an overhead trolley, with an underrunning trolley wheel—the system of power supply ultimately to become almost universal. The line employed a 2,000-volt DC current with the return of power through the rails. In this second summer, management of the line was taken over by J. J. Wright, the general manager of the Toronto Electric Light Company, who had been active in getting the project under way. His chief problem was in finding men willing to work the motor car with its noise and continued shooting of sparks, and most of the time he operated the car himself from morning till late at night. But once again the operation was regarded as a great success and one of the highlights of the fair. Seventy thousand passengers were carried without an injury—although one day the train, when running backward, derailed and went over the embankment onto the Grand Trunk tracks. It was picked up by a group of men and placed back on its track.[1]

Despite numerous favourable references by the Toronto newspapers, there was no suggestion that electric cars might replace the city horse-car lines, and even Wright expressed misgivings about the feasibility of operating electric cars on crowded city streets. The cars continued to operate each summer until the King Street city line was extended to the Dufferin Street entrance of the Exhibition in 1892. Meanwhile, several persons who had seen the line in operation became interested in the possible use of electric cars in their home cities, and promoted the making of arrangements with Van Depoele for such installations. Late in 1885 he completed electrification of the Montgomery, Alabama, city system, the first electrified transit system of any size. Notwithstanding the success of the trolley wheel at the Toronto Fair, Van Depoele had continued to attempt to use a troller similar to that of the Daft system, but he finally shifted to the trolley wheel in Montgomery, with the return of current through the rails.

There were still many technical difficulties in the way of entirely successful operation, and it was neither Daft nor Van Depoele who solved these, but Frank Sprague, a graduate of the United States Naval Academy, who had experimented actively with applications of electricity while in the naval service. Upon his resignation from the Navy in 1883, he worked for a time with Thomas Edison, but left after a year— Edison was always suspicious of college-trained men—and set up his own company to produce electrical equipment. He developed not only a greatly improved motor, but also the system of placing the motors under the cars and gearing them directly to the axle, but supporting them by springs. This became the standard technique. His electrification of the Richmond, Virginia, lines in 1887 resulted in the first large city electric railway in the United States, and its immediate success led to a rapid expansion of the Sprague system, which largely replaced Daft and Van Depoele installations. The Sprague enterprise was absorbed by General Electric, but Sprague remained active in the field until his death in 1934.

In the early period of development, there was much interest in electric street car operation in Detroit. After an unsuccessful Van Depoele experiment in 1885, service was established in 1886 on Woodward Avenue, first with third rail, and then with overhead trolley. In the same year the Port Huron system was electrified. Interest spread across the river, and on May 28, 1886, the first commercial electric railway in Canada commenced operation on $1\frac{1}{2}$ miles of track in Windsor. This was a Van Depoele installation, costing a reported $8,500. The history of the line during its early years is obscure, but electric operation did experience difficulties and for a time was suspended in favour of horse cars. Eventually, in the early nineties the system was rebuilt and electrification extended.

Meanwhile, at the other end of southern Ontario, in 1887, electrification of the little St. Catharines city system was undertaken, and with it the seven-mile intercity route to Thorold, which had been built in 1881 as a horse-car route with grades up to $7\frac{1}{2}$ per cent. On October 5 regular service commenced on the line, the first intercity electric railway in Canada. This was also a Van Depoele operation, with twelve cars and speeds up to fifteen miles an hour. Again the early history is obscure, but, as far as is known, electric operation was continuous from the date of establishment.

These early cars used the troller system, with two trolley wires, one negative, the other positive. But because the troller had an unfortunate habit of coming off the wires and clattering on to the roof of the car, to the annoyance of the passengers, it was soon replaced with a single trolley pole, rail-return-of-power system.

In the next decade the use of the electric street car spread rapidly; lines in several cities were electrified before 1890, and on August 15, 1892, the first electric line in Toronto (Church Street) was placed in operation. The electric car soon replaced horse cars, and the electric lines were extended to serve new areas. Ultimately, forty-six cities, plus adjacent suburbs, had street railway service.

Atlantic provinces: Halifax, Moncton, Saint John, St. Stephen, Sydney, Yarmouth, and St. John's, Newfoundland.

Quebec: Hull, Levis, Montreal, Quebec City, Sherbrooke, Three Rivers.

Ontario: Belleville, Brantford, Cornwall, Fort William, Guelph, Hamilton, Kingston, Kitchener, London, Niagara Falls, Oshawa, Ottawa, Peterborough, Port Arthur, Sarnia, St. Catharines, St. Thomas, Sault Ste. Marie, Sudbury, Toronto, Waterloo, Welland, Windsor.

West: Brandon, Calgary, Edmonton, Lethbridge, Moose Jaw, Nelson, Regina, Saskatoon, Vancouver (including North Vancouver and New Westminster), Victoria, Winnipeg.

Some lasted only a few years (for example, Belleville) but the majority continued for several decades. Most of the larger systems were in operation until after World War II, and Montreal and Ottawa lines lasted until 1959. By 1965 only Toronto still retained street car operation. The history of these urban lines is a major undertaking in itself; the present volume is confined to the intercity routes.

## THE DEVELOPMENT OF THE INTERCITY LINES

With the perfection of the street railway, increased attention was given to the possibility of using electric power for transportation between cities and towns as well as within the cities. By 1890 most of the settled areas of Canada were well supplied with steam railroad service that provided adequate transportation for longer distance travel. But there was still a great need for improved facilities for movement from farm or village to nearby cities, and for frequent service between adjacent cities. For the farmer, direct rail service was not available, except after a drive by horse and buggy to the nearest station. Even for travel between nearby towns and cities where rail service was available, the infrequency of schedules and the usually inconvenient location of stations made the service inadequate in terms of the needs. For this type of travel, much of it for shopping, working in a nearby city, visiting friends or relatives, or attending school, church, or meetings, frequency of service was of utmost importance. Similarly, steam railroad service was unsuited for many commercial travellers who sought to visit a number of towns each day. It was into this vacuum that the electric railway moved. Although it could never meet the needs perfectly— particularly those of farmers not fortunate enough to be located close to the lines— it represented a major step, and had its development not been cut short by the motor vehicle its accomplishments would have been far greater.

The expansion of the industry following the original Thorold line was slow at first (Table I). The initial lines were confined primarily to relatively densely settled areas, which clearly offered the best potentialities. One of these areas was the section westward from downtown Vancouver, and in 1891 a line was completed to New Westminster via Central Park, the first in the ultimately extensive network of British

Columbia Electric. The next line was unique, in that it was designed primarily for sightseers, in this instance, to the Niagara Falls area. It was placed in operation in 1893 between Niagara Falls and Queenston, and a few years later extended across the river on bridges at each terminus, to permit the loop operation which for the next three decades was to serve thousands of tourists. The highly industrialized Grand River valley attracted electric railway builders, and in 1894 a line was completed from Galt to Preston. In 1896 came the Hamilton, Grimsby and Beamsville, running beside the road down through the orchards of the Niagara fruit country. Hull Electric placed a line to Aylmer (Quebec) in operation in 1897, involving electrification of a Canadian Pacific branch. The pre-1900 period also saw the beginning of the Toronto area lines. In 1889 the Metropolitan Railway had electrified its Yonge street line to Eglinton—essentially as a street car route, but the line soon took on interurban characteristics as it was extended to Richmond Hill in 1896 and to Newmarket in 1899. The Weston, High Park and Toronto, later Toronto Suburban, which had great ambitions, had managed to reach Weston by 1893, and 1894 saw service established to Long Branch by the Toronto and Mimico line.

These pre-1900 lines were for the most part built along the highways; there was little grading; sharp curves were frequent; and standards of operation were essentially

TABLE I

MILES OF INTERCITY ELECTRIC RAILWAY LINE COMPLETED BY YEAR IN CANADA

| Year | Miles | | Year | Miles | |
|------|-------|---|------|-------|---|
| 1887 | 7 | | 1908 | 78 | |
| 1888 | 0 | | 1909 | 6 | |
| 1889 | 2 | | TOTAL 1900–9 | | 364 |
| TOTAL before 1890 | | 9 | 1910 | 77 | |
| 1890 | 3 | | 1911 | 23 | |
| 1891 | 12 | | 1912 | 5 | |
| 1892 | 0 | | 1913 | 53 | |
| 1893 | 22 | | 1914 | 37 | |
| 1894 | 4 | | 1915 | 31 | |
| 1895 | 0 | | 1916 | 76 | |
| 1896 | 34 | | 1917 | 49 | |
| 1897 | 30 | | 1918 | 0 | |
| 1898 | 0 | | 1919 | 0 | |
| 1899 | 14 | | TOTAL 1910–19 | | 351 |
| TOTAL 1890–99 | | 119 | 1920 | 0 | |
| 1900 | 26 | | 1921 | 0 | |
| 1901 | 27 | | 1922 | 0 | |
| 1902 | 21 | | 1923 | 0 | |
| 1903 | 28 | | 1924 | 2 | |
| 1904 | 40 | | 1925 | 7 | |
| 1905 | 43 | | 1926 | 4 | |
| 1906 | 18 | | TOTAL after 1919* | | 13 |
| 1907 | 77 | | | | |

SOURCE: Data compiled for individual roads. When lines were previously operated by steam power, date given is that of electrification. Dates are given for year in which regular service started.

* No mileage was built after 1926.

those of the street railways. They were little more than rural trolley lines—street car routes operating out into rural areas. The cars, however, were larger than earlier models and speed had been increased. The total mileage in operation in January 1900 was 128.

The first decade of the century was the period of most rapid expansion, just as it was in the United States. Projects sprang up all over the country, charters were obtained, and 359 miles of line were placed in service during the decade, nearly half of the total ultimate mileage. In the first part of the decade, about twenty-five miles a year were completed. The rural street car technology gradually gave way to that of the distinctly different intercity electric line. More private rights of way were utilized instead of operation alongside highways. New lines had less severe grades and less curvature, and cars were built specifically for higher-speed intercity operation, although the transition was not complete until after 1906. Among the lines opened during the first part of the decade were the little Woodstock, Thames Valley and Ingersoll, a side-of-the-road operation (1900), the Sydney and Glace Bay (1902), the line from Windsor to Amherstburg, the extension of the Galt-Preston line to Berlin (Kitchener), the Grand Valley's line from Brantford to Paris and Galt, and the Pictou County line through the industrial area around New Glasgow in Nova Scotia. In 1906 Hamilton Radial completed its line to Oakville, and in 1906 and 1907 the South Western Traction's line from London via St. Thomas to Port Stanley was placed in operation.

Mileage completed had jumped sharply in 1905, but 1907 and 1908 saw the peak amounts, both over seventy-five miles, as well as the first of the high-speed lines on private rights of way comparable in technology to the midwest interurbans in the United States. The Chatham, Wallaceburg and Lake Erie completed its main line in 1908; the Windsor, Essex and Lake Shore was finished in 1907 and 1908, and the Brantford and Hamilton as well as the Winnipeg–Selkirk in the latter year. Meanwhile, Toronto and York Radial had reached Lake Simcoe in 1907, the new portion of its line being clearly interurban in character. Much of the mileage of British Columbia Electric was completed in this period, as well as that of the Niagara, St. Catharines and Toronto, the first section of which was electrified in 1900. This road also absorbed the pioneer line to Thorold.

In the development in this decade, one very sharp contrast with the United States is noted. The peak year for new building in the United States was 1903, and the most concentrated period of building was 1901–4. In Canada there was no comparable boom in these early years, the peak occurring in 1906–9 at the same time as the second but less important major period of building in the United States. About 12,000 miles were placed in operation in the United States in this decade, or three-fourths of the total ever built, whereas in Canada less than half the total was built in this decade.

After a temporary fall to six miles of new line in 1909, a result largely of the financial difficulties of 1907 which curtailed new projects, construction was renewed on an extensive scale in 1910. Although the new mileage was only five in 1912, in the following five years a total of 246 miles was placed in service. With seventy-six miles, 1916 was the third most important year in the industry. The United States was again a contrast because, although there was considerable building in the years 1910–14, the annual amount was less than half that of the peak years, and in 1918 and 1919 fell off to negligible figures. The major Canadian route completed in 1910 was British Columbia Electric's Fraser Valley line. The road's Burnaby line was finished in 1911,

B

and the Saanich line on Vancouver Island in 1913. The Nipissing Central was completed in 1914; in the summer of 1915 electric operations commenced on the rebuilt London and Port Stanley, one of Canada's pioneer steam roads. Lake Erie and Northern electrification was completed the following year, most of the track having been placed in operation with steam power in 1915. In the period 1913–17 the Montreal and Southern Counties finished its line to Granby, one projected for over a decade. And in 1917 at long last the Toronto Suburban opened service to Guelph; most of the work had been finished three years before but the war delayed completion. With this line, construction was virtually at an end. In the twenties only two minor lines were placed in service, both involving electrification of steam trackage—the Montreal and Southern Counties' Marieville–Ste Angele line, and the Merritton–Port Dalhousie line of the Niagara, St. Catharines and Toronto. In this abrupt ending the Canadian experience paralleled that in the United States where only a negligible amount, less than 200 miles, was built after 1918.

The routes built after 1910 were more characteristically interurban than the 1900–10 lines, with private rights of way, high-speed equipment largely of steel construction, and the handling of carload freight service. The London and Port Stanley, rebuilt and electrified by the city of London under the initiative of Sir Adam Beck, represented the highest stage of development of the electric railway in Canada, a model of what later construction would have been if all expansion had not been cut short by the rise of the motor vehicle.

### THE COMPLETED SYSTEM

The total mileage built in Canada was 856, but not all of this was in operation in any one year. The London and Lake Erie (South Western Traction) and the Grand Valley had been abandoned before the last lines were placed in operation. The bulk of the total, 553 miles, was concentrated in Ontario. Of this, 137 miles were in the Toronto area, with lines radiating out to Lake Simcoe, Guelph, and suburban areas in Scarborough and Long Branch. A partially built line eastward to Oshawa and Bowmanville was never operated. Hamilton had four lines with 78 miles radiating outward to Beamsville (and, for a few years, on to Vineland), to Brantford, to Oakville, and a short route to Dundas. Slightly less was the Niagara–St. Catharines area mileage of 74, which connected with the New York state lines. The Grand River valley lines totalled 89 miles. There were two lines between Brantford and Galt, but the portion of one line north of Paris was abandoned when operation of the other commenced. The London area had 52 miles, consisting of two parallel lines to Port Stanley, one of which was abandoned soon after the second was completed. There were 97 miles of line in the Windsor and Chatham areas. The most isolated line was the little Nipissing Central in the New Liskeard area.

The Quebec mileage of 91 miles consisted of three roads, extending outward from Hull, Montreal, and Quebec respectively; most of the travel was of suburban nature. There were only two lines in the Maritimes, both in Nova Scotia, with a mileage of 37. One was in the mining and steel area of Cape Breton, the other around New Glasgow. There were only two systems in all western Canada, one north from Winnipeg to Selkirk, the other the British Columbia Electric. The latter, the largest single system in Canada, with 138 miles of line, was partly suburban in character, but also had one long line up the Fraser valley, and a disconnected line on Vancouver Island.

The Ontario lines, although more complete than those in the other provinces, in no sense constituted an integrated network. The Hamilton lines connected with those in the Grand Valley, but otherwise each group of lines was distinct. The most obvious gap was the eleven-mile stretch through level country from Oakville to Port Credit. Closing of this would have provided a Toronto–Hamilton line, but little through business would have been possible without substantial reconstruction of the lines to allow higher speed. Another was the six-mile link from Vineland to St. Catharines, which would have joined the Hamilton and Niagara lines. If these two gaps had been closed, it would have been possible to go by electric railway, for example, from Guelph to virtually any city in upstate New York or the entire midwest of the United States, in fact as far as Freeport, in western Illinois, or Sheboygan, Wisconsin. Another gap in the Canadian roads was from Bridgeport to Guelph, which separated Toronto Suburban from the Grand Valley lines.

### Time Necessary for Construction

Data relating dates of incorporation and completion of the lines are available for seventeen companies. Most of the other lines were converted from steam or horse to electric operation, and thus no suitable figures can be ascertained. In a number of cases one segment of the line was placed in commercial operation before the entire road was completed. Accordingly, Table II provides two tabulations, one for the lapse of time from date of incorporation to that of placing the first segment in operation, the second for completion of the entire line as contemplated when construction was started, or as much of it as was ever completed. The four- to five-year period constitutes both the median and the mode in both columns. However, when the entire line is taken into consideration, a larger number of companies took ten years or more. Montreal and Southern Counties took twelve years to get its first segment into operation, and nineteen years to reach Granby, still many miles short of its destination of Sherbrooke. Toronto Suburban took twenty-seven years to reach Guelph; Winnipeg, Selkirk and Lake Winnipeg fourteen years to reach Stonewall; and Hamilton Radial thirteen years to reach Oakville. Only Woodstock, Thames

### TABLE II

LAPSE OF TIME BETWEEN INCORPORATION AND COMPLETION OF LINES

| Years between incorporation and operation | Number of companies | |
|---|---|---|
| | First segment in operation | Final portion in operation |
| Less than 2 | 3 | 3 |
| 2–3 | 4 | 2 |
| 4–5 | 7 | 7 |
| 6–9 | 2 | 1 |
| 10 and over | 1 | 4 |

Valley and Ingersoll placed the first segment (five miles) of its line in operation in the same year in which it was incorporated.

The reasons for the delays were obvious. Obtaining rights of way was often a slow task and the raising of money was frequently difficult. In some instances, delay occurred in obtaining rails and equipment. The typically long period, relative to the small size of the undertakings, was a major factor in the difficulties experienced by new enterprises attempting to get on their feet.

## The Unbuilt Lines

Of the twenty-three companies for which information on their proposed systems is available, nine completed the lines that were indicated in their charters or published plans, although some of these companies may at times have given consideration to extensions that were never built. Two others, the Lake Erie and Northern and the Woodstock, Thames Valley and Ingersoll, completed their original plans except for minor branches, although the latter road was soon conceived of as a link in a longer system.

Of the other twelve companies, some completed the basic part of the planned network, as, for example, the Windsor, Essex and Lake Shore and the Chatham, Wallaceburg and Lake Erie. A few, such as Toronto Suburban, did not reach their original destination but did ultimately build lines of substantial length. But others, such as Hamilton Radial, Grand Valley, and London and Lake Erie never built more than small fractions of their planned routes. The following list indicates planned but never attained destinations of the major lines of the companies, as set out in the original incorporating legislation or early amendments:

Windsor, Essex and Lake Shore—Leamington to Chatham.
Chatham, Wallaceburg and Lake Erie—to Petrolia, Dresden, Blenheim.
Hamilton, Grimsby and Beamsville—to St. Catharines, Niagara Falls.
Hamilton Radial—from Hamilton to Guelph and Mount Forest, and to Berlin (Kitchener) and Elmira.
Grand Valley—Port Dover to Brantford; Galt to Berlin and Goderich; and Guelph to Elora. A few years later the plan was alterd completely, with plans for the line to go west from Paris to London.
Grand River—Waterloo to Goderich.
South Western Traction (London and Lake Erie)—London to Hamilton. Plans were soon changed to provide for a line from Aylmer to St. Thomas and London, with a branch to Port Stanley. The portion from London to Port Stanley was built.
Toronto and York Radial—Toronto to Stouffville and to Bowmanville; Toronto to Hamilton; Toronto to Barrie.
Toronto Suburban—Toronto to Hamilton and Niagara Falls.
Niagara, St. Catharines and Toronto—St. Catharines to Toronto; Niagara Falls to Fort Erie.
Montreal and Southern Counties—Granby to Sherbrooke.

In addition to these uncompleted lines of intercity companies, several of the street car enterprises planned intercity routes which they never built. The major ones, excluding  purely suburban operations, were:

Guelph Radial—Guelph to Hespeler and Berlin.
Niagara, Welland and Lake Erie—Welland to Niagara Falls and Port Colborne. The city portion was built as a segment of the planned interurban line rather than as a street railway as such.
Oshawa Railway—originally planned as a steam road, from Oshawa via Lindsay to the Chalk River area.
Peterborough Radial—Peterborough to Lakefield and Stony Lake, and to Bridgenorth.

Finally, there were numerous companies that did not build any portions of projected lines (Table III). As noted in part II there were several roads on which substantial work was done and rails laid but operation never commenced. Toronto Eastern and Ontario West Shore are the prime examples. On others such as the People's Railway west from Guelph and the Dunnville, Wellandport and Beamsville, some grading was undertaken. But many companies never even commenced construction. Most were in Ontario and had they all been completed, there would have been a continuous interurban line from Windsor via Toronto to Cornwall and Ottawa, with branches to Stratford, Niagara, Orillia, Lindsay, Peterborough, and other towns. There were few serious projects outside of Ontario; a line would have connected Moose Jaw and Regina, for example; another Brandon, Virden, and Souris; a third, Sherbrooke and Quebec.

Most of the authorized but unbuilt lines were within the realm of reason, although many would clearly have been unprofitable. One, however, was little short of fantasy: the Boynton Bicycle Electric Railway Company was chartered in 1894 to build a monorail electric line from Winnipeg via Toronto, Ottawa, Montreal, and Saint John to Louisburg in Nova Scotia with a branch to Quebec City. The Boynton Bicycle system was tested on a mile track at Hageman Station on Long Island, New York, in the summer of 1893.[2] On the basis of contemporary descriptions, which are somewhat obscure, it would appear that the cars operated on two wheels of five feet in diameter, one attached to each end of the car, and running on a single rail. A small wheel at the top of the car collected power from an electrified rail, and also maintained balance. The double-track line was built with two 12-inch logs set 8 feet apart on the ground and held together by ties; on each log a rail was placed. Posts extending 11 feet above ground were placed between the logs, and the upper rail was fastened to cross arms placed on these posts. Unlike the usual monorail, the weight-bearing rails were the lower ones. The cars were to be 51 feet in length, 7 feet 6 inches high, and 4 feet wide. Speeds of 100 miles an hour were claimed. Fortunately, the Canadian line was never built.

In addition to the companies actually chartered, hundreds of projects were promoted and noted in the trade journals, but never reached the charter stage.

### PROMOTION AND CONTROL

Promotion of the lines came from various sources. Some were initially local enterprises, such as the Windsor, Essex and Lake Shore and the Lake Erie and Northern. But most were promoted by Canadian or United States syndicates, and those which were locally promoted usually fell into syndicate hands. The Haines syndicate of New York, for example, electrified and rebuilt the Niagara, St. Catharines and Toronto and attempted to build the Hamilton–Brantford line. The Von Echa Company, with its headquarters in Harrisburg, Pennsylvania, and represented in Canada by Dr. S. Ritter Ickes, built the Grand Valley and the Woodstock, Thames Valley and Ingersoll, and initiated the Brantford and Hamilton, all as parts of a major projected network. Most of the lines ultimately, and often quickly, passed out of the hands of the original promoters into the control of other groups. In turn through bankruptcy or other changes, control often shifted again. As a consequence, it is difficult to present a systematic tabulation of ownership patterns.

In the years prior to World War I, the most significant name in the industry was

## TABLE III

### LINES INCORPORATED BUT NEVER BUILT*

| Name of company | Major projected lines | Date of incorporating act |
|---|---|---|
| *Ontario* | | |
| Belleville Radial Ry.† | Belleville–Shannonville | 1909 |
| Brantford and Erie Ry. | Brantford–Port Dover | 1904 |
| Buffalo, Niagara and Toronto Ry. | Niagara-on-the-Lake–Fort Erie–Port Colborne–Welland; St. Catharines | 1906 |
| Cobourg, Port Hope and Havelock Electric Ry. | Port Hope–Cobourg | 1909 |
| Cobourg Radial Ry. | Cobourg–Peterborough | 1909 |
| Dunnville, Wellandport and Beamsville Elec. Ry. | Port Maitland–Beamsville; Port Dover–St. Catharines | 1906 |
| Eastern Ontario Elec. Ry. | Cornwall–Toronto | 1909 |
| Hamilton, Ancaster and Brantford Ry.‡ | Hamilton–Brantford | 1896 |
| Hamilton, Waterloo and Guelph Ry. | Hamilton–Galt–Waterloo; Hamilton–Guelph–Elora | 1906 |
| Humber Valley Elec. Ry. | Lambton Mills–Toronto | 1912 |
| Ingersoll Radial Elec. Ry. | Ingersoll–Tillsonburg | 1897 |
| International Radial Ry. | Fort Erie–Hamilton–Waterloo–St. Marys; Meaford; Goderich | 1895 |
| Kingston, Gananoque and Perth Elec. Ry. | Kingston–Gananoque–Perth–Arnprior | 1895 |
| London, Aylmer and North Shore Elec. Ry. | London–Port Burwell | 1901 |
| Middlesex and Elgin Interurban Ry. | London–Aylmer | 1902 |
| Morrisburg and Ottawa Elec. Ry. | Morrisburg–Ottawa | 1908 |
| Mt. McKay and Kakabeka Falls Ry.§ | Kakabeka Falls–Fort William | 1904 |
| Niagara, Queenston and St. Catharines Ry. | St. Catharines–Niagara–Queenston | 1903 |
| North Midland Ry. | London–Clinton–Mitchell; London–Stratford | 1904 |
| Ontario Electric Ry. | Cornwall–Toronto | 1902 |
| Ontario–Michigan Ry. | Sarnia–Chatham–Windsor** | 1911 |
| Ontario West Shore Ry. | Goderich–Owen Sound; Goderich–London | 1902 |
| Ottawa and St. Lawrence Elec. Ry. | Lancaster–Cornwall–Brockville–Perth; Brockville–Morrisburg–Ottawa | 1909 |
| Ottawa, Brockville and St. Lawrence Ry. | Ottawa–Brockville | 1900 |
| Owen Sound and Meaford Ry. | Owen Sound–Meaford | 1905 |
| People's Ry. | Woodstock–Kitchener–Guelph–Elora–Arthur | 1909 |
| Petrolea Rapid Ry. | Sarnia–Courtright–Petrolia | 1902 |
| Porcupine Rand Belt Elec. Ry. | Lines in Porcupine mining area | 1912 |
| Rainy River Radial Ry. | Fort Frances–Lake of the Woods | 1910 |
| St. Joseph and Stratford Elec. Ry. | St. Joseph–Stratford | 1904 |
| St. Thomas Radial Elec. Ry. | St. Thomas–Port Stanley; St. Thomas–Wallacetown–Rodney; St. Thomas–Aylmer–Port Burwell | 1895 |
| Simcoe Ry. and Power Co. | Penetanguishene–Midland | 1909 |
| Smiths Falls, Rideau and Southern Ry. | Smiths Falls to Merrickville; Smiths Falls–Gananoque | 1898 |
| South Essex Elec. Ry. | Windsor–Amherstburg–Leamington–Point Pelee | 1896 |
| Stratford Radial Ry. | Stratford–St. Marys–Embro | 1903 |
| Stratford and St. Joseph Radial Ry. | Stratford–St. Joseph | 1907 |
| Sudbury and Wahnapitae Ry. | Sudbury–Lake Temagamingue | 1899 |
| Tillsonburg and Southern Counties Radial Ry. | Port Burwell–Tillsonburg–Woodstock | 1909 |
| Toronto Barrie and Orillia Ry. | Toronto–Barrie | 1910 |
| Toronto Eastern Ry. | Toronto–Cobourg; to Peterborough and Lindsay | 1910 |
| Toronto, Hamilton and Niagara Falls Elec. Ry. | Toronto–Niagara Falls | 1895 |

TABLE III (*continued*)

| Name of company | Major projected lines | Date of incorporating act |
|---|---|---|
| Toronto Interurban Ry. | Toronto–Newmarket | 1911 |
| Toronto, Niagara and Western Ry. | Toronto–Hamilton–Niagara | 1903 |
| Welland and Port Colbourne Ry. | Welland–Port Colborne | 1926 |
| Windsor, Chatham and London Ry. | Windsor–London | 1906 |
| *Quebec* | | |
| Co. du Chemin de Fer Elec. des Trois Rivieres, etc. | Three Rivers–Maskinonge | 1905 |
| Quebec District Ry. Co. | South from Levis | 1895 |
| Quebec Eastern Ry. | Sherbrooke–Quebec City | 1907 |
| Three Rivers and North Shore Elec. Ry. | Three Rivers–Montreal | 1898 |
| Vercheres, Chambly and Laprairie Tramways | Longueuil–Laprairie and Boucherville | 1916 |
| *Prairie Provinces* | | |
| Alberta Interurban Ry. | Calgary–Medicine Hat; Banff; Lethbridge | 1911 |
| Alberta Metropolitan Ry. | Calgary–Shepherd | 1911 |
| Brandon Elec. Ry. | Brandon–Souris–Minnedosa–Neepawa | 1911 |
| Brandon Rural Radial Ry. | Brandon–Souris, Neepewa, Minnedosa, Rapid City, Virden | 1913 |
| Edmonton Interurban Ry. | Edmonton–Morinville, Fort Saskatchewan†† | 1910 |
| Edmonton Northwestern Radial Ry. | Edmonton–Pembina River | 1914 |
| Edmonton, Stony Plain and Wabamun Ry. | Edmonton–Stony Plain | 1913 |
| Lacombe, Bullocksville and Alix Elec. Ry. | Lacombe–Alix | 1907 |
| Lethbridge Radial Tramway | Lethbridge–Raymond–Stafford | 1907 |
| Maharg Elec. Ry. | South from Calgary | 1911 |
| Manitoba Radial Ry. | Winnipeg–Portage–Stony Mt. | 1911 |
| Manitoba Radial Ry. Co. | Winnipeg–Lake Winnipeg | 1907 |
| Red Deer Ry. | Red Deer–Nevis | 1907 |
| Regina Interurban Tramway | Regina–Lumsden | 1908 |
| Regina–Moose Jaw Interurban Ry. | Regina–Moose Jaw | 1912 |
| Selkirk Elec. Ry. | Winnipeg–Selkirk | 1892 |
| *British Columbia* | | |
| Bassano and Bow Valley Ry. | Bassano–Bow Valley | 1911 |
| Crows Nest and Prairie Elec. Ry. | Crows Nest Lake–Pincher Creek | 1907 |
| Crows Nest Pass St. Ry. | Cowley–Crows Nest Lake | 1911 |
| Kaslo and Slocan Tramway | Kaslo–Bear Lake | 1893 |
| *Transcontinental* | | |
| Boynton Bicycle Elec. Ry. (monorail line) | Winnipeg–Louisburg, Nova Scotia‡‡ | 1894 |

\* Unbuilt electric roads for which charters were granted as listed in the Department of Transport volume, *A Statutory History of Steam and Electric Railways in Canada, 1836–1937* (Ottawa, 1938), and *Appendix* (Ottawa, 1954). The list is probably not entirely complete, and in some instances it was difficult to tell if electric power were intended or not.

† Eventually built as a private electric freight line from the Belleville Portland Cement Company plant at Point Anne to the Grand Trunk Railway.

‡ The Brantford and Hamilton built this line after the HA&B failed to complete construction.

§ A five-mile line out of Fort William was built and operated by steam power in freight service.

\*\* Including a car ferry to interchange equipment with Michigan Railways at Port Huron.

†† Part of this line was built and operated with gas-electric cars.

‡‡ So far as can be ascertained, no unbuilt intercity electric railway projects were incorporated in the Maritime provinces, except the Boynton line.

that of Sir William Mackenzie. Together with his associates—his construction partner Sir Donald Mann; Frederick Nicholls, president of Canadian General Electric; E. A. Wood, Toronto financier and YMCA enthusiast; banker Aemilius Jarvis, and others—he ultimately gained control over five of the larger companies (Toronto and York Radial, Toronto Suburban, the Niagara, St. Catharines and Toronto, the Winnipeg, Selkirk and Lake Winnipeg, and the Chatham, Wallaceburg and Lake Erie), and thus of more than one-fourth of the interurban mileage, as well as the Toronto and Winnipeg city systems and some mileage in the United States. A farm boy from Kirkfield, north of Lindsay, Mackenzie passed from rural school teacher and house builder to railroad contractor, railroad promoter, and one of Canada's great entrepreneurs in the period of the country's most rapid expansion. He had a great flair for obtaining capital for his enterprises from other people, building the $400-million Canadian Northern entirely with borrowed money and government aid. Unfortunately, his interests were too widespread to allow him to concentrate much attention on his electric railways, and such plans as he had for extending them were finally ended by the development of the Ontario Hydro-Electric railway projects, and by the collapse of the Canadian Northern as World War I cut off the supply of funds needed to finish it. Most of his interurbans ultimately ended up in public hands.

A much smaller network was controlled by G. B. Woods in the period after 1908, consisting of the former Von Echa properties and the London and Lake Erie. These were all weak lines, and the inability of the owners to complete connecting links, plus the development of strong competitors, resulted in early destruction of the roads.

The bonds of many of the companies, particularly the Mackenzie lines, were sold largely in Great Britain. However, British interests developed and controlled only two properties, the big British Columbia Electric and the South Western Traction (later London and Lake Erie). Likewise, despite substantial American promotion of the early enterprises, few remained under American control. Two, however, were direct subsidiaries of American transit lines: the Niagara Falls Park and River was a portion of International Railway of Buffalo, and until 1920 Sandwich, Windsor and Amherstburg was a Detroit United property (itself owned in some measure by Canadians, but controlled by the Everett-Moore syndicate, one of the largest promoters of electric railways in the United States). Sydney and Glace Bay (Cape Breton Electric) was a Stone and Webster property, the only Canadian line which was directly controlled by an American holding company, although for a short time Winnipeg Electric and its interurban subsidiary were partially controlled by the Insull group. Canadian General Electric aided in the financing of a few companies, including Grand Valley, but never gained control of them. CGE's president, Nicholls, was a director of a number of the electric roads, primarily the Mackenzie lines, and a promoter of the Buffalo, Lockport and Rochester in New York state.

The four electric roads out of Hamilton were all ultimately controlled by Dominion Power and Transmission Company, which also owned Hamilton Street Railway. Dominion, an outgrowth of the Hamilton Cataract Power Light and Traction Company, was promoted by local Hamilton business men. British Columbia Electric and the Winnipeg lines were also affiliated with power and transit interests; and all three of these ultimately fell into the hands of the Power Company of Canada, Limited, a Canadian holding company controlled by the Nesbitt-Thomson interests. The Mackenzie properties also integrated interurban, transit, and power interests, as did the Cape Breton company noted above and Quebec Railway, Light and Power.

Three companies were controlled throughout most of their lives by the Canadian Pacific: the Grand River, the Lake Erie and Northern, and the Hull Electric (until 1926). The first of these, one of Canada's earliest lines, was acquired by the CPR before 1900, and the Lake Erie and Northern, promoted by Brantford business men, was purchased by the CPR before it was completed. The greatest railway-owned mileage, however, was that of the Canadian National, consisting of three of the Mackenzie properties acquired with the Canadian Northern, the Grand Trunk's Montreal and Southern Counties, and the Quebec Railway line which the Canadian National purchased in 1951. With the Grand Trunk also came the Oshawa Railway, an urban transit system with important switching and terminal lines. Nipissing Central was owned almost from the beginning by the Temiskaming and Northern Ontario (now the Ontario Northland). Thus about 300 miles or nearly 40 per cent of the total eventually fell into railroad hands.

In sharp contrast to the picture in the United States, more than half of the total mileage in Canada eventually was taken over by governmental units. This includes, of course, the CNR and the Temiskaming and Northern Ontario lines noted above. In addition, from its inception the London and Port Stanley was owned largely by the city of London, and a total of 200 miles eventually passed into the hands of the municipal authorities or the Ontario Hydro-Electric Power Commission.

## CHAPTER TWO

# PHYSICAL PLANT AND OPERATION

## TRACK AND ELECTRIC POWER

THE CONSTRUCTION STANDARDS for the electric railways varied widely, as they did in the United States. The first lines were built to street car standards along the sides of roads, with substantial curvature and grades in some instances, and—the eternal plague of the roadrunners—the great number of driveway crossings. Most of these lines were never rebuilt to higher standards. The Hamilton, Grimsby and Beamsville, most of the London and Lake Erie, and the earlier segments of Toronto and York Radial were good examples of this type of construction. At the other extreme were the electrified steam lines such as the London and Port Stanley which had been built as main line railroads with grades and curvature held to a minimum. At an intermediate level were such lines as the Windsor, Essex and Lake Shore, the Guelph line of Toronto Suburban, and the Port Colborne line of the Niagara, St. Catharines and Toronto, all built as electric roads, but primarily on private rights of way. Canadian lines possessed two of the steepest grades on electric lines in North America; Toronto and York Radial's Lake Simcoe line climbed out of Hogg's Hollow on the northern outskirts of Toronto on an 8-per-cent grade, and the original line of British Columbia Electric into New Westminster entered the latter town on a 12-per-cent grade. This segment was later relocated. Except in suburban areas, the lines were all single track.

The earliest lines were laid with iron rail, and the Galt, Preston and Hespeler had some in service even after 1900. However, the majority of lines were laid with steel rails. The lightest was the 50-pound rail on the Port Dalhousie, St. Catharines and Thorold, and on the Hamilton, Grimsby and Beamsville, but the most common was 56 pounds in weight, much of it kept in service till the end of operations. This included the Grand Valley, the Galt, Preston, and Hespeler, the Hamilton Grimsby, and Beamsville, the Woodstock, Thames Valley and Ingersoll, and Toronto and York Radial (earlier lines). Another group, including such roads as the Pictou County, the Sydney and Glace Bay, and the South Western Traction used 60-pound rail. Roads designed for carload freight service, including the Niagara, St. Catharines and Toronto, the London and Port Stanley, the Lake Erie and Northern, and others, used rails of 80-pound weight, typical of steam railroad branch lines, and some had sections of even heavier rail.

All of the roads were built to the standard gauge of the railroads, 4 feet $8\frac{1}{2}$ inches, with two exceptions: Sydney and Glace Bay used the gauge, 4 feet 7 inches, of the Sydney city system, and the Toronto area roads used the broad gauge, 4 feet $10\frac{7}{8}$ inches, of the Toronto transit system. Both the latter gauges, of course, precluded handling of steam road cars. The Metropolitan (Lake Simcoe) line was eventually converted to standard gauge, then converted back to city gauge in 1927. The Long Branch line was converted to standard in 1922 and back to city in 1927. The Scarborough line was always city gauge. Toronto Suburban also converted ultimately to standard, from its initial 4 feet $10\frac{1}{2}$ inches.

In all cases, electric power was supplied to the cars by overhead trolley wire; there were no third-rail lines in Canada as in the United States, where about a dozen of the interurbans used this source of power. Most of the Canadian lines used a single directly supported trolley wire, but the Grand River and some of the later roads, including the Windsor, Essex and Lake Shore, the London and Port Stanley, the Lake Erie and Northern, and one line of the Niagara, St. Catharines and Toronto, employed catenary construction where the trolley wire was suspended from a steel cable. The Windsor, Essex and Lake Shore prior to 1929 and the London and Port Stanley used pantographs with a bar contacting the trolley wire, and the other roads the usual pole trolley.

Several lines generated their own power initially and often sold some power for other uses. Others relied on commercial sources, and as time passed more shifted over to the relatively cheaper hydro electric power. In Ontario by 1929 only the Windsor, Essex and Lake Shore was still generating its own power, the dynamos in the Kingsville power plant driven by ancient steam engines. Power was transmitted by all roads at high-voltage AC to substations, located at intervals of from ten to fifteen miles along the line, where it was converted to DC and fed into the power lines. Low-voltage DC cannot be carried longer distances without substantial loss of power. 600-volt DC was the standard power for street railways and for most of the interurbans in the United States and Canada, but as lines grew in length the voltage drop and need for substations created additional costs, and led to a search for a superior method. Around the turn of the century, particularly in Europe, there was substantial experimentation with alternating current for operation. The Ganz electrical firm in Budapest developed one system which the South Western Traction attempted to use when it built southward from London in 1902. But various technical difficulties led to its replacement by standard 600-volt DC operation early in 1907.

In the years immediately after 1900, the single-phase AC system was developed, promoted particularly by Westinghouse, and adopted, to their later regret, by a number of United States lines. The Windsor, Essex and Lake Shore was built with this system, utilizing 6,600 volts directly on its cars. Although single-phase AC eliminated line drop and the need for frequent substations, it greatly increased the weight of the cars and resulted in much higher costs for maintenance of electrical equipment. In addition the cars had a much slower accelerating speed. Many United States roads shifted over to DC after two or three years, but the Windsor, Essex and Lake Shore continued with AC until it was modernized in 1929.

By 1910 another alternative to low-voltage DC had been developed, namely, the use of DC at relatively higher voltages. This was more successful than AC and was adopted at 1,500 volts by the London and Port Stanley, the Lake Erie and Northern, and the Toronto Suburban's Guelph line. To facilitate interchange of equipment, Lake Erie and Northern's affiliated Grand River shifted from 600 to 1,500 in 1921.

## Passenger Equipment

A wide variety of passenger equipment was employed. The cars of the pioneer Thorold line were tiny units of street car design, seating about twenty, and the original Hamilton, Grimsby and Beamsville cars were 28 feet long. The other early lines used cars of 30 to 40 feet in length, seating from twenty-five to forty passengers. As early as 1901, however, the Niagara, St. Catharines and Toronto purchased cars of typical

United States interurban design of the period, 50 feet in length, and capable of speeds up to 50 miles an hour. Most of the cars built from 1905 to 1913 were from 45 to 55 feet long with an average seating capacity of around fifty, although some used on the light-traffic lines or in suburban service were less than 40 feet. Windsor, Essex and Lake Shore's six heavy cars built in 1908 were 55 feet in length, and the Brantford and Hamilton cars exceeded these by a foot. After 1913 there was a noticeable increase, most of the cars exceeding 50 feet, including the eight cars of the Lake Erie and Northern and the five cars of the London and Port Stanley, built in 1916, with 59-foot length and capacity of seventy passangers. Eleven cars for the Lake Erie and Northern and the Grand River, built in 1920, were 61 feet 8 inches, and Toronto Suburban's nos. 107 and 108, built in 1924, were 61 feet 9 inches long with a capacity of sixty-six. Among the largest cars ever built in Canada, so far as is known, were the six steel cars ordered by Quebec Railway in 1929, 65 feet in length and a capacity of seventy-four, and cars nos. 12 and 14 of London and Port Stanley, built in 1917, 71 feet 7 inches long and weighing 51 tons. All the cars built after 1916 and many earlier ones remained in service as long as the lines provided passenger service. The last regular passenger cars to be built were four for the rebuilt Windsor–Leamington line in 1929. In 1947 the last piece of interurban passenger train equipment, a baggage-passenger combine, was built for Grand River Railway as car no. 626.

Two companies built most of the interurban cars. The oldest of these was the Ottawa Car Company, established in 1891. It produced a large portion of all Canadian street cars as well as a number of interurban cars, from some of the earliest units down through the heavy cars of the Windsor, Essex and Lake Shore in 1907 to the Quebec Railway's and WE&LS's cars in 1929. The other company that built a high percentage of the Ontario intercity cars was the Preston Car and Coach Company of Preston, Ontario, founded in 1908. From 1921 until its liquidation in 1923, it was a subsidiary of J. G. Brill Company of Philadelphia, a major United States producer of electric cars. Preston built for the lines in the Grand Valley, the Toronto Suburban, the Chatham–Wallaceburg line, the Hamilton lines, and others. A few cars were built by the Niagara, St. Catharines and Toronto and the British Columbia Electric in their own shops, and a few by other companies, including Patterson and Corbin, the Tillsonburg Electric Car Company, and National Steel Car Company which built part of the Montreal and Southern Counties equipment.

Inevitably some cars were imported from the United States. Brantford and Hamilton cars were built by Kuhlman, a major Ohio car manufacturer, and British Columbia Electric purchased a number from Niles, American, and other United States firms. London and Lake Erie also acquired Niles cars, and the London and Port Stanley motor cars were built by Jewett, another Ohio firm. So far as is known, the only line to acquire British-built cars was the South Western Traction, which was initially financed and built by British interests. Various lines at times purchased second-hand United States cars; Nipissing Central acquired several cars from the East St. Louis, Columbia and Waterloo when its own were destroyed by fire, and Cape Breton Tramways in later years acquired several relatively modern cars from the Greenfield and Montague Transportation Area in Massachusetts when the latter shifted to buses in the early thirties. London and Port Stanley used four cars from the Milwaukee Electric system, three of which had once been parlour cars. Brantford and Hamilton obtained three cars from Cincinnati and Columbus Traction Company, Toronto and York Radial several from Norwich and Westerly in Connecticut and from Lehigh Valley Transit Company.

Car designs varied somewhat over the years, being influenced by both street car and railroad passenger car development. Virtually all cars built prior to 1912 and many built thereafter had monitor roofs in the style of older railroad coaches, with small ventilation windows on the vertical segments of the upper portions. Following the trend in the United States, some of the later cars built for Toronto Suburban, British Columbia Electric, Quebec Railway, the Sandwich, Windsor and Ahmerstburg, and the Windsor, Essex and Lake Shore had arched roofs. Some cars were combination express and passenger cars, particularly those used on light-traffic lines, but most were straight passenger cars, usually with two compartments, smoking and non-smoking. The larger roads had separate express cars. Virtually all cars were built for two-man operation, with entrance and exit of passengers at the rear. One exception was the group of cars built for Toronto Suburban in 1917, with centre doors, the conductor being located in the middle. Two of these were destroyed by fire in the Preston car shops just before they were to be shipped to Toronto Suburban. The parlour cars commonly used on major United States lines were almost unknown in Canada, except for the one car built for the Windsor–Leamington line at the time of its reconstruction in 1929. This car had a solarium with large lounge chairs. Diners and pullmans, used on some United States lines, were likewise unknown in Canada, because of the shortness of the routes. The majority of cars had their own motors. The earliest cars had two 25- or 30-horsepower motors; by 1900 four motors were common, at first with 50 horsepower and in later years with 75 to 85. The larger roads had some motorless trailer cars. Most lines ultimately had equipment designed for multiple-unit operation, whereby one motorman controlled the power in all motor cars.

The earlier cars were of wooden body construction, with steel underframing. After 1916, most of the new cars were steel, although Montreal and Southern Counties had wooden sheeted cars built in 1922 because of the weight restriction on the Victoria Bridge. The steel cars reduced the accident hazard, but were substantially heavier. The London and Port Stanley motor cars weighed 92,920 pounds and the 1929 Quebec Railway cars 85,000, compared to the typical figure of around 40,000 for the earlier wooden cars. The modern lightweight steel car era that dominated the United States interurban car building in the twenties bypassed Canada almost entirely. Four cars built for the modernized Windsor–Leamington line in 1929 were of modern semi-streamlined design but at 34 tons were not technically lightweight. These eventually went to Montreal and Southern Counties and then to the Niagara, St. Catharines and Toronto, where, in March 1959, two of them, nos. 620 and 623, made the last scheduled intercity electric railway passenger runs in Canada. A series of lightweight steel suburban cars was built by Ottawa Car Company in 1924 and 1925 for Ontario Hydro's radial operations, a portion going to the Windsor–Amherstburg line, and the remainder first to the Mimico line and then to the North Yonge segment of the Toronto and York Radial.

As suggested above, a substantial shifting of cars from one line to another occurred. For example, four cars built by Preston in 1914 for the Edmonton city system ended up back in Ontario; two provided service for a number of years on the Scarborough line of the Toronto and York Radial, and the other two came to Oshawa Railway. When the latter line discontinued passenger service in 1940, the cars went to the Niagara, St. Catharines and Toronto, where they served until 1950. This road also acquired two cars from the abandoned Eastern Ohio Traction; one of these, originally no. 107, built in 1924, made the last passenger run on the Toronto Suburban in 1931, then went back to the NStC&T as car no. 83 where it operated for nearly thirty additional years. It made most of the runs the morning that the NStC&T discontinued passenger service in March 1959.


## FREIGHT EQUIPMENT

The early interurbans were built primarily for passenger service, but most of them soon turned to freight operation. The roads fell into two groups so far as freight activities were concerned. One confined its operations to package merchandise freight, and for this service typically used cars built to much the same specifications as the passenger cars. Some were motor cars, some trailers. The other group of roads, although handling package freight, stressed carload freight traffic, using standard railroad cars drawn by electric freight motor cars. Some of the motor cars resembled passenger cars, but most were built specifically for freight train operation, and contained no space for carrying goods. Some roads, particularly British Columbia Electric, had a number of their own cars, but many used primarily the freight cars obtained in interchange from the steam roads.

The type of freight handled varied widely. The primary commodity on the Fraser line of British Columbia Electric was lumber; on the Hamilton, Grimsby and Beamsville, fruit from the Niagara Peninsula; on the London and Port Stanley, coal from the lake carriers to London; and on the Winnipeg–Selkirk line, milk. For a time during prohibition days in the United States, the Sandwich, Windsor and Amherstburg reportedly did a thriving business in beer which it delivered to the Detroit River for smuggling to the United States.

As in the United States, the lines suffered from numerous car barn fires. Grand River lost its barns and most of its cars in 1906, and South Western Traction suffered the same fate the following year. British Columbia Electric lost its New Westminster barns in 1904, Nipissing Central both its barn and cars in 1917, and Toronto and York Radial both its Metropolitan and Scarborough division car barns in 1918.


## PASSENGER OPERATIONS

The standards of operation, speed, frequency of service, and so on varied among the roads and over the years. One major characteristic was the relatively high frequency of service—the great inherent advantage of electric power, which permitted small-unit operation, in contrast to steam-powered trains. Many roads established service on a uniform basis—hourly, for example—rather than at non-uniform intervals as is typical of the railroads. This was, of course, of great convenience to the traveller. Two-hour intervals were common. In a few instances, however, only a few runs a day were operated: the Fraser Valley line of British Columbia Electric provided only three trains a day, and Quebec Railway scheduled trains on irregular frequency intervals. At the other extreme, the suburban lines out of large cities often operated at intervals of less than an hour, as low as every fifteen minutes on British Columbia Electric's high density main line to New Westminster. Table IV gives a sample of service frequencies for 1920 and 1930, showing that there was very little change over this decade. The table indicates the basic schedule, but on some lines there were additional runs in rush hours, and less frequent service at night and often on Sundays.

TABLE IV

INTERVALS OF OPERATION OF ELECTRIC LINES, 1920 AND 1930

| Company | Line | Service interval* | |
|---|---|---|---|
| | | 1920 | 1930 |
| Brantford and Hamilton | entire | hourly | 2 hr. |
| Grand River | Galt–Preston | 30 min. | 30 min. |
| | Galt–Kitchener | hourly | hourly |
| Lake Erie and Northern | entire | 2 hr. | 2 hr. |
| London and Port Stanley | London–St. Thomas | hourly | hourly |
| | St. Thomas–Port Stanley | 2 hr. | hourly |
| Windsor, Essex and Lake Shore | entire | 2 hr. | 2 hr. |
| Niagara, St. Catharines and Toronto | St. Catharines to: | | |
| | Port Dalhousie | 30 min. | 45 min. |
| | Merritton | 30 min.† | 3 trains‡ |
| | Niagara Falls | hourly | hourly |
| | Port Colborne | hourly; 90 min. | hourly |
| | Niagara-on-the-Lake | hourly | 5 trains |
| British Columbia Electric | New Westminster main line | 15 min. | 15 min. |
| | Burnaby | hourly | hourly |
| | Lulu Island | hourly | hourly |
| | Fraser Valley | 3 trains | 3 trains |
| | Saanich | 6 trains | 6 trains |
| Toronto Suburban | main line | 2 hr. | 2 hr. 20 min. |
| Montreal and Southern Counties | Montreal–Marieville | n.a.§ | 11 trains |
| | Marieville–Gramby | n.a. | 5 trains |
| | Montreal South | n.a. | 20 min. |
| | Ste Angele | n.a. | 3 trains |
| Niagara Falls Park and River | entire | 40 min. | 30 min. |
| Quebec Railway | Quebec–Ste Anne de Beaupré | 8 trains | 11 trains |

*Where trains are indicated, the number given is per day.
†Thorold–McKinnon, on old line.
‡Merritton–Port Dalhousie line.
§n.a.—not available.

The roads that continued service down to the post-World War II period typically reduced the number of trains somewhat, although several lines, and particularly British Columbia Electric, operated much the same service until the time of discontinuance. By 1954 Lake Erie and Northern was down to four trains each way daily, and London and Port Stanley to six trains.

Much of the service on most lines was provided by single-car trains, and some roads, such as Hamilton Radial, lacked equipment capable of multiple-unit operation. On other roads, two-car trains, one often a trailer, were not uncommon, and British Columbia Electric frequently operated three-car trains on the Fraser Valley line. Several lines operated much longer trains, up to five cars or more at times, particularly those roads handling substantial resort or week-end traffic, with its peak load on Sunday evening. On rare occasions, some roads, including British Columbia Electric, pulled passenger trains with electric freight motors.

The nature of the passenger business varied with the roads. With all lines the bulk of the travel was short distance in nature—shoppers or workers going to the nearest city from farm, village, or town. An additional portion consisted of shopping, business, or visiting travel between nearby cities—Brantford and Hamilton, London and St. Thomas, for example. On the inner portions of the lines a substantial commuter travel was built up, a forerunner of the extensive commuting from suburb or farm to city by bus and automobile in subsequent years. Some lines carried large numbers of school children. Several depended heavily upon tourist or resort travel. The Toronto and York Radial carried a heavy volume of summer traffic to Lake Simcoe points, and many a Torontonian of today recalls the Sunday evening trips back to the city, the cars jammed with picnic baskets and luggage. The London and Lake Erie and then the London and Port Stanley handled substantial travel to the beach at Port Stanley, and Hamilton Radial did so on the short run to Hamilton Beach. Winnipeg, Selkirk and Lake Winnipeg likewise carried important week-end traffic. The travel of pilgrims to the Catholic shrine at Ste Anne de Beaupré was an important source of revenue for the Quebec Railway, and Niagara Falls Park and River was almost exclusively a tourist facility. Niagara, St. Catharines and Toronto likewise handled a substantial tourist business, in part in conjunction with its steamers from Toronto to Port Dalhousie.

Several roads provided connections for main line trains. London and Port Stanley offered a connection to London for Michigan Central passengers, and operated some of its trains into the steam road's ancient brick station in St. Thomas. The Lake Erie and Northern and the Grand River provided connections for Canadian Pacific trains into the CPR station in Galt, as well as to their own station downtown. Niagara, St. Catharines and Toronto provided train connections at Merritton for Welland and Port Colborne. Other lines served areas having little or no main line railroad services—the two Windsor roads, the Chatham, Wallaceburg and Lake Erie, and the Quebec Railway, for example. Many of the Ontario roads cut across the main lines, providing the only north-south service. But others paralleled steam roads and competed actively for the passenger traffic—the Brantford and Hamilton and Toronto Suburban, for example.

So far as speed was concerned, the interurban cars were capable of maintaining a much higher level than operating conditions permitted. Although the first cars to operate on the Thorold line were capable of only 15 miles per hour, by 1900 speeds up to 50 were readily attained, and the later equipment would attain 70 or more. But on most lines the frequency of stops and the condition of the grade and track prevented an average speed of more than 30 miles an hour. In 1904, for example, reported figures show an average speed of 15 for the Grand Valley, the Hamilton, Grimsby and Beamsville, and the Woodstock, Thames Valley and Ingersoll, 25 for Hamilton Radial, 30 for Niagara, St. Catharines and Toronto, 21 for Quebec Railway interurban lines, 10 for Sydney and Glace Bay, and 26 for South Western Traction (1906). The London and Port Stanley, with its good track and equipment, normally required about 35 minutes to make the 16-mile run from London to St. Thomas; and the Niagara, St. Catharines and Toronto required 35 minutes for the 13-mile run from St. Catharines to Niagara, and 51 minutes for the 19-mile run to Port Colborne. Speeds averaging around 40 miles an hour were planned on the projected Hydro radial network around Toronto (discussed in chapter V). On most lines station stops were frequent, and trains would stop at virtually any cross road on signal.

Station facilities varied with the line and the size of city. There were only a very few relatively imposing city stations, the best example being the union terminal on King Street in Hamilton, used by the four lines of Dominion Power. Built in 1907 at a cost of $250,000, the facilities included a substantial office building and ticket office. This building stood until 1959. A covered train shed was planned but never

Hamilton Radial Railway no. 305. This car was originally built in 1906 for the Brantford and Hamilton by the Ottawa Car Company. The 57-foot, 28-ton car was scrapped in 1933 (Photograph from collection of J. Wm. Hood).

British Columbia Electric Railway no. 1301. Canada's most westerly interurban, the British Columbia Electric Railway, used heavyweight wooden cars, such as the one pictured here at New Westminster, British Columbia. (Photograph by Peter Cox.)

Electrified at 1500-volt, D.C. in 1915, the London and Port Stanley purchased a series of heavy steel cars from Jewett for use on the 24.5-mile line. They saw continuous service until the end of passenger service in the mid-1950's. (Photograph by J. Wm. Hood.)

Grand River Railway no. 844. Seen here at Galt, this car is typical of the heavyweight cars operated by the Canadian Pacific on their subsidiaries, the Grand River and the Lake Erie and Northern railways. These cars, weighing 52 tons, were powered by four 125-horsepower motors and were built in 1921. (Photograph from collection of J. A. Brown.)

Niagara, St. Catharines and Toronto Railway no. 83. This car, originally no. 107 on the Toronto Suburban Railway, was one of the cars sold to the NStC&T on the abandonment of the former line. On the latter, it was used until the cessation of passenger service in 1959. Built in 1924, it was 61 feet 9 inches long. (Photograph by J. Wm. Hood.)

Quebec Railway, Light and Power Company no. 452. This car was built by the Ottawa Car Company in 1930, and is seen here as it turned on the reversing wye at Montmorency Falls, Quebec. (Photograph from collection of J. A. Brown.)

Windsor, Essex and Lake Shore Railway no. 505. In 1930 the WE&LS purchased five cars of this design from Ottawa Car. After only two years' use on that line the cars were sold to the Montreal and Southern Counties Railway, where they ran until 1955. Four of these, the most modern electric interurban cars ever built in Canada, finished their life on the Niagara, St. Catharines and Toronto, being scrapped in 1960. (Photograph from collection of C. S. Bridges).

Canadian National Railways no. 17. This freight motor, built in 1918 by National Steel Car for the Ontario Hydro, later saw service on the Niagara, St. Catharines and Toronto and finished its days on the Oshawa Railway. (Photograph by J. Wm. Hood.)

built. British Columbia Electric had a somewhat similar facility in downtown Vancouver in conjunction with the company's office building. But the typical station was a much smaller facility. Wayside stations were small wooden structures designed merely to provide protection from the elements. In some towns stores served as ticket agencies. London and Port Stanley used the Canadian National station in London, the Niagara–St. Catharines line the parent road's station in Port Colborne, and Toronto Suburban the CNR station in Guelph. The Grand River and the Lake Erie and Northern shared a station in downtown Galt, and the latter road one with the Brantford and Hamilton in Brantford. In Port Dover the Lake Erie and Northern operated over a mile of electrified CNR track to reach that road's station.

One of the major problems of the lines was that of reaching the downtown areas of cities in satisfactory fashion; it was important for them to get close to the business area if they were to meet the needs of their patrons. The cars commonly ran on the streets, either on street railway track or the line's own rails laid in the streets. The London and Lake Erie passed through St. Thomas on the tracks of the local street car system, and street running was to be found in Windsor, Kingsville, Leamington, Chatham, Toronto, Hamilton, Sydney, and elsewhere. Street running had its hazards, particularly after the growth of the automobile, and even in smaller cities the expense of paving, usually placed on the company, became substantial. Some cities ultimately forced lines to suspend operations by driving them off the streets, as was true in Chatham and Merritton, for example. In Toronto the interurban lines from Lake Simcoe and Guelph never reached the downtown area. The Simcoe line terminated at various successive points on Yonge Street, ultimately at Deloraine Avenue, just south of Hogg's Hollow, where a transfer could be made to city cars. This feature, of course, greatly reduced the usefulness of the line. The plans of Sir Adam Beck for a system of radial lines called for a high-speed private right of way to the downtown area. The former steam roads, particularly the London and Port Stanley and Quebec Railway, had private right of way lines into the downtown areas of the cities served, but the numerous grade crossings reduced speed.

## OPERATING HAZARDS

In addition to automobiles, as noted above, there were other operating hazards such as the lack of adequate signalling systems. Only the roads built or rebuilt at a late date had adequate electric block signals. Others had either no signals and thus operated on train orders, always a potential danger with frequent service, or street car type signal systems, which were adequate for ordinary purposes, but were not foolproof. The roads were extremely lucky in avoiding major head-on collisions. Although some did occur, such as the crash of two Windsor, Essex and Lakeshore cars in a heavy fog three miles south of Windsor on November 15, 1923, the one really serious accident, described on page 93, involved a runaway car on a steep grade.

Heavy storms were more of a hazard for electric roads than for steam because of damage to the power lines. Few of these were serious enough to be reported, but when they did occur they were a nuisance to the passengers. The Chatham, Wallaceburg and Lake Erie was shut down by snow for several weeks in February 1918, for example, and the great snow of 1912 virtually put the impoverished Grand Valley out of business; their cars did not operate for several months.

c

## CHAPTER THREE

# ECONOMIC SIGNIFICANCE OF THE LINES

THE ECONOMIC EFFECTS of the electric lines in Canada were confined to relatively small areas; had the roads been extended as the promoters had planned, similar to development in the midwestern United States, the effects would have been far greater. In general, the electric lines were significant in beginning a trend that the motor vehicles were to carry to completion—the shift in intercity travel from reliance upon the infrequent schedule and the fixed and infrequent stop pattern of the steam railroads to types offering greater flexibility in the form of more frequent operation and more convenient stopping. With smaller and relatively inexpensive units and small crews, the electric cars could be run economically at much more frequent intervals than the steam trains, and, with their ability to operate on city streets and close to highways, they could reach more convenient locations. Electric power also facilitated frequent stops. As compared to the other alternative, the horse and buggy, the electric railway was much faster, more dependable, and more convenient.

One consequence was a great increase in the mobility of the rural and village population in the areas served. Shopping trips to nearby cities became more feasible and much more frequent; the electric car started the trend away from village and small town shopping that the automobile was to carry much further. Commercial travellers could reach more customers, and business and professional men could conduct their activities in other cities much more conveniently.

In the areas of larger cities, the electric lines, just as the city street car routes, increased the size of the area in which commuting to work was feasible, and thus lessened housing congestion in downtown areas. In some areas the lines also increased the possibility of beach and lake recreation, and the Simcoe line, particularly, greatly increased the trend towards summer cottage and resort vacations. Students in rural areas were enabled to attend high schools in nearby towns more easily, and Catholic pupils to attend separate schools. In some sections the trend towards school consolidation was aided by the electric roads.

Just as the lines increased the mobility of persons, likewise they facilitated the handling of merchandise freight, offering much greater flexibility and speed than the steam lines. The service was particularly important for perishables, such as vegetables, fruit, ice cream, milk, and cream, for newspapers, and for repair parts. This type of freight was often handled on the passenger cars, or on separate trains operated on passenger train schedules. A small town retailer could telephone in an order to a supplier in the morning and obtain delivery on the noon train, whereas several days might have been required by steam road freight service. The electric lines offered few advantages so far as carload freight was concerned, except their ability to reach certain points near the downtown areas.

Unfortunately for the electric railroad, all of its advantages were possessed by the motor vehicle to a much higher degree, once the latter was perfected and highways built. Accordingly, the electric line, as an intermediate step in the direction of flexibility, was ultimately destroyed by the form of transport that carried its advantages much farther. Only in one aspect did the electric railway have any long-range benefits, namely, for heavy volume passenger traffic into large cities on private rights of way. This advantage became more significant as street congestion grew, but few of the Canadian electric lines possessed high-speed entrances into downtown areas, as did some of their United States counterparts.

## CHAPTER FOUR

# GOVERNMENT REGULATION AND ASSISTANCE

As COMMON CARRIERS doing a general business of transportation for the public and frequently using public property such as streets, the intercity electric railways were subjected to control over the their activities by the various levels of government—Dominion, provincial, and local. The sphere of Dominion control was much greater than that of Federal control in the United States. The electric railways in Canada received a certain amount of financial assistance in the form of government subsidies, and, particularly in later years, a number of the lines passed into government ownership.

## DOMINION VERSUS PROVINCIAL CONTROL

The line between provincial and Dominion control was much more sharply drawn than that between state and federal control in the United States. The Dominion Board of Railway (later Transport) Commissioners had exclusive jurisdiction (with minor exceptions provided by certain legislation) over two sets of railways: those incorporated under Dominion legislation, such as Nipissing Central, and those incorporated by provincial legislation but declared by an act of Parliament to be a "work for the general advantage of Canada." Most of the electric lines were ultimately subject to such legislation, and in effect provincial control was limited to a few that were not, of which the major examples were the Hamilton and Dundas, the Hamilton, Grimsby and Beamsville, the Sandwich, Windsor and Amherstburg, and the Niagara Falls Park and River.

Although there was little dispute over jurisdiction, certain questions did arise. Some of the difficulty was created by a clause of the Railway Act of 1903 which provided that, when a provincially incorporated line crossed or connected with a line subject to the jurisdiction of Parliament, the provincial line was a work for the general advantage of Canada so far as the connection, crossing, or through traffic was concerned. In an early case, this rule was interpreted as not giving to the Board of Railway Commissioners the power to require the electric line to install sidings on its line for the benefit of through shipments. The major case, however, arose out of an order of the Ontario Railway and Municipal Board that the Hamilton, Grimsby and Beamsville instal toilet facilities on its cars (see *Re Ross and Hamilton, Grimsby and Beamsville Ry. Co.*, 25 DLR 613, 1916). The line claimed to be exempt from Ontario control because of both the crossing provision noted above, and a Dominion order in 1895 authorizing it to cross the Grand Trunk. The Ontario Supreme Court, in a decision upheld by the Judicial Committee of the Privy Council (29 DLR 521), ruled that the crossing provision did not make the line subject to Dominion control except for the matters relating to the crossing itself, and thus it was not exempt from provincial control.

By specific provision of the Dominion legislation, there were certain exceptions to the Dominion's exclusive jurisdiction over lines subject to its control. The major one gave precedence to provincial legislation relating to Sunday operation of cars, except on certain lines. In 1897, Ontario enacted legislation prohibiting the operation of electric cars on Sunday. The Dominion Railway Act of 1903 provided that incorporation of a road by the Dominion or declaration that it was a work for the general advantage of Canada did not exclude it from Lord's Day legislation, unless it operated in two or more provinces or to the United States. In 1912, the London and Lake Erie, a road for which Sunday operation was very important because of its excursion business to the lake, was held by the Ontario courts (*Kerley* v. *London and Lake Erie Transportation Co.*, 14 CRC 111) to violate the provincial legislation. The court said that the road was not operated as a part of a through route to the United States, and that the Lord's Day legislation was valid because it related to railway operation and did not involve criminal law (which is restricted to the Dominion). On appeal to the Ontario Supreme Court, however, the law was held not to apply to electric railroads that were not under the exclusive jurisdiction of the province. But not until Ontario legislation on the subject was liberalized in 1913 was general Sunday operation on intercity lines possible. Even then progress was slow; only in 1915 was Toronto Suburban authorized to provide general Sunday service. One bit of irony in the situation was the fact that in several instances the demand for Sunday operation came from persons who wished to use the cars to attend church—and of course, the leaders of the movement for restrictve legislation were predominantly from church organizations.

There was some uncertainty for years over the precise status of control of British Columbia Electric. In a 1922 case, *Hunting Merritt Lumber Co. et. al.* v. *British Columbia Electric Railway Co.* (28 CRC 121), the Board of Railway Commissioners noted that BCE had not been declared to be a work for the general advantage of Canada, and thus its freight rates were not subject to Dominion jurisdiction. However, in 1929, in *Canadian Pacific and British Columbia Electric Ry. Cos.* v. *Canadian National Rys. et. al.* (36 CRC 263), the Board held that BCE was subject to Dominion jurisdiction by nature of its operations, and upheld a previous order requiring the establishment of through rates with the CNR.

## MUNICIPAL CONTROL

The use of public roads and streets necessitated local franchises from the cities and rural townships involved. Sometimes a popular vote of the ratepayers was necessary for the granting of the franchise. These franchises set up obligations for paving, and in some instances established maximum fares on a zone or per mile basis. As paving techniques improved and became more expensive, the roads objected to being required to meet these higher standards, and in some instances their objections were upheld by the provincial or Dominion authorities.

There were a number of disputes over the franchise fare requirements at the end of World War I when, although costs of operation rose rapidly, the fares were frozen. For lines subject to provincial control, the provincial governments could and in some cases did override the municipally imposed franchise requirements. For example, Ontario legislation authorized the Hamilton, Grimsby and Beamsville to exceed its franchise fare requirement. For lines subject to Dominion control, the Board of

Railway Commissioners also was held to have the power to override the franchise fare limits. This rule was established in the case of *Montreal and Southern Counties Ry. Co.* v. *Towns of Greenfield Park et. al.* in 1916 (23 CRC 106) and upheld by the higher courts. It was employed in a number of subsequent cases, including ones involving the Nipissing Central in 1921 and the Niagara, St. Catharines and Toronto in 1926. There was, however, one exception to this rule, namely, when the act incorporating the enterprise or declaring it to be a work for the general advantage of Canada contained a statement that franchise rules took precedence. The major case involved the Hamilton Radial, which sought fare increases in 1918 that would exceed the franchise limits. In *Hamilton Radial Electric Co.* v. *City of Hamilton, et. al.* (23 CRC 114), the Board of Railway Commissioners held that it could merely authorize increases in such cases subject to franchise revision; it could not order an increase which would override the franchise rules.

Questions arose also with regard to the termination of franchises. Power of a municipality to compel forfeiture for violation of charter provisions was upheld, even when the line was subject to Dominion control, in *City of Brantford* v. *Grand Valley Ry. Co.* in 1913 (15 DLR 87), the case arising over the failure of the road to provide service. Likewise the power of municipalities to require abandonment of lines upon expiration of the franchise, even though the company was under Dominion control, was upheld in 1931 when the right of the town of Merritton to require the Niagara, St. Catharines and Toronto to remove its St. Catharines–Merritton local line when the franchise expired was sustained (*Merritton* v. *Niagara, St. Catharines and Toronto Ry. Co.*, 38 CRC 227). Parliament could undoubtedly have prevented such action by legislation, but did not chose to do so. Lines subject to Ontario control were protected against such action by provincial legislation; the Merritton case was complicated by the claim of the railroad that a provision of the relevant 1914 township by-law stated that the rules of the Province of Ontario Railway Act were binding on the company, and thus that the provision of such legislation preventing municipalities from forcing abandonment of lines was applicable. The Board of Railway Commissioners held that it was not; the by-law did not (and could not) transfer the line from Dominion to provincial jurisdiction, and thus Ontario legislation was not relevant.

Although the municipalities were anxious to encourage the building of the intercity lines, their subsequent attitude towards them varied widely. The early enthusiasm and support often waned. For years the city of Toronto carried on a bitter battle with all Mackenzie properties, harrassing them in every way possible with little regard for the users of the service. Windsor followed a similar policy for a time, and Chatham finally forced the Chatham, Wallaceburg and Lake Erie out of business.

## REGULATORY POLICIES

Within their respective spheres, the Board of Railway Commissioners and the provincial authorities exercised control over matters of rates and service. Maximum per-mile-fare rules were set by law and cases arose only when a company wished to exceed either the general figure or a fare that had been approved specifically for the company. For many years, the Dominion legal maximum was 3 cents a mile, while the Ontario provincial figure was 2 cents. Most of the cases arose shortly after World War I when costs rose sharply, and in several instances careful review of costs and revenues was made. In 1918, in *Re London and Port Stanley Ry. Co.* (14 CRC 160), a 15-per-cent rate increase was allowed because of demonstration of higher costs. Similarly, increases were allowed for the Montreal and Southern Counties in 1918, and for Nipissing Central in 1921.

There were a few cases involving freight rates, but the policies followed were the same as those for steam roads. There were only a few cases involving joint rates and interchange with steam roads, an issue of major concern in parts of the United States. In 1916 in *London and Lake Erie Ry. Co.* v. *Michigan Central and London and Port Stanley Ry. Cos.* (20 CRC 194), the Board of Railway Commissioners required the Michigan Central to sell through tickets in conjunction with the London and Lake Erie at St. Thomas, as it already did with the London and Port Stanley. In the same year, in *Brantford Manufacturers* v. *Lake Erie and Northern Ry. Co.* (31 CRC 1), the board required interchange between the Lake Erie and Northern and the steam roads (Toronto, Hamilton and Buffalo and Grand Trunk) at Brantford, over the objections of the latter roads, in order to allow direct access by the CPR (owner of the LE&N) to Brantford manufacturing plants. In 1949, however, in *Port Dover* v. *C.N.R. and Lake Erie and Northern Ry. Co.* (63 CRC 350), the board refused the request of Port Dover to order re-establishment of interchange and of a switching agreement in Port Dover, which had been eliminated in 1947 when the Lake Erie and Northern ceased operating over CNR tracks in the village. In one major case in 1929, British Columbia Electric was required to establish joint rates with the CNR—the reverse of the typical order—over CPR opposition.

Frequency of service, provision of stations and stops, and safety matters were also subject to control. On various occasions lines were required to provide additional stops, or increase train frequency; thus British Columbia Electric was required to increase service on the Burnaby line to thirty-minute intervals in 1929.

Control over construction was maintained through provisions of the acts incorporating the enterprises, and thus by direct legislative action. However, new lines subject to Dominion control could not be operated until certified by the Board of Transport Commissioners. The board had no control over abandonment of lines until 1933, and thus some electric lines were discontinued without the need for official sanction. When passenger service alone was discontinued, however, action was required; an early case of this sort was that of the Chatham, Wallaceburg and Lake Erie in 1928 (*Township of Dover* v. *Chatham, Wallaceburg and Lake Erie Ry. Co.*, 34 CRC 116). The board refused to order the line to restore passenger service because of the sharp drop in passenger traffic prior to discontinuance and the poor financial condition of the company, despite some inconvenience, especially to school children, resulting from abandonment. One exception to the rule that abandonment did not require approval was the case in which the original franchise or charter contained the requirement that certain service be provided. When the city of Toronto abandoned the Schomberg line in 1929, it was notified by Dominion authorities that this action was illegal in light of the fact that the original subsidy grant was contingent upon the operation of two trains a day. The city rejected the argument and the Dominion did not press its case.

In the later years of the industry a number of cases involving abandonment of lines or of passenger service came to the Board. In a few instances the right to abandon was initially denied. In *Lake Erie and Northern and Grand River Railways* v. *Township of Port Dover et. al.* (65 CRC 124), in 1950, the application of these two lines to discontinue passenger service was denied because of public inconvenience that would result. The total traffic, about 2,100 persons a day, was substantial, and although a loss was being incurred on this service the operation of the lines as a whole, including freight service, was profitable. When British Columbia Electric applied to abandon its Steveston line passenger service in 1952 (69 CRC 220), permission was granted only for the Vancouver–Marpole section, but denied beyond Marpole because of the problems of traffic congestion on the streets.

In most abandonment cases, however, permission was granted. This was true with Hull Electric's Aylmer line in 1946 (60 CRC 196), and the 1955 application of the Grand Valley lines (in *Discontinuance of Passenger Train Service, Lake Erie and Northern and Grand River Railways*, 72 CRC 290). Continued loss of traffic since 1950 and heavy out-of-pocket losses were considered to outweigh the inconvenience to the users of the services. Montreal and Southern Counties was permitted to abandon passenger service in 1955, subject to some temporary restrictions, because of bridge reconstruction (*Re Montreal and Southern Counties R. Co. Abandonment*, 73 CRC 131). It was allowed to abandon its Ste Angèle branch (74 CRC 186) because the annual freight traffic of about twenty cars did not warrant rebuilding the line for diesel operation. In *Re London and Port Stanley Railway Passenger Service* (74 CRC 295), in 1957, this road was permitted to abandon service in light of a $6,000 monthly out-of-pocket loss, the refusal of the voters of London to approve funds for rehabilitation of the line, the sharp decline in traffic over the past five years, and the availability of bus service. The losses were considered to outweigh inconvenience to the 1,800 passengers a week still using the service.

A similar position was taken in *Re CNR Commutation Service, Montmorency Subdivision*, in 1959 (78 CRC 257), the board noting the sharp decline in traffic, mounting losses, the wearing out of equipment, and the availability of bus service. And finally, in 1959, in *Re CNR Passenger Train Service, Port Colborne–Thorold* (78 CRC 204), permission was granted to abandon this last operation, because the savings to the company would outweigh any inconvenience that might result to the public. The sharp drop in traffic (350,000 passengers in 1953 to 95,000 in 1957), the heavy out-of-pocket losses, and the need for substantial reinvestment to keep the equipment operating were noted as reasons for approving abandonment.

Both provincial and Dominion incorporation was provided by action of the legislative bodies, not by administrative agencies as in the United States, Authorizing legislation sometimes contained fare restrictions and other controls not frequently found in the United States. These were of course subject to change by subsequent legislative action.

## Financial Assistance

To a greater extent than in the United States, electric lines were given financial aid, primarily by the municipalities through which they built, in the form of some type of cash subsidy. Thus, for example the Hamilton, Grimsby and Beamsville was given a subsidy of $25,000 by the city of Hamilton when it was built in the nineties. The Chatham, Wallaceburg and Lake Erie received $35,000. Such grants were almost non-existent in the United States. The Dominion government gave financial aid to several lines, as it did to steam roads, usually to the sum of $7,500 a mile. For example, Lake Erie and Northern received $320,191, Schomberg and Aurora $46,144, Quebec Railway, $96,000, and Niagara, St. Catharines and Toronto $38,400.

## CONTROL OF MOTOR CARRIER COMPETITION

As truck and bus lines developed, the electric lines began to seek protection from them, turning to the provinces because intra-provincial motor carriers were not subject to Dominion control. In 1923, Ontario legislation gave to the Minister of Public Works and Highways the power to regulate motor buses. The actual policy determined by the Minister, George Henry, changed materially over the period between 1923 and 1926. Initially, he indicated that he could not restrict bus competition with the radials, because "the people demand it [bus service]."[1] However, by 1925, he had commenced to change his attitude materially, when he prevented bus competition with the Brantford–Paris line and the Metropolitan Division. In 1926 he announced a very specific policy: no competition would be permitted with the radials so long as their service was adequate. In some instances, established bus lines were required to withdraw from service upon improvement of electric rail service, as in the case of the Toronto–Weston line. As a consequence of the restrictive policy, most of the Ontario radials were protected from direct bus competition, and their life prolonged somewhat. Several lines (the Grand River, the Brantford and Hamilton, and the Windsor, Essex and Lake Shore, for example), started or acquired bus subsidiaries in order to protect themselves. Other provinces were slower to act, but Quebec established a policy similar to that of Ontario in 1926. British Columbia Electric, the only large system outside Ontario and Quebec, had been subject to bitter "jitney" competition on its New Westminster route. BCE's own co-ordinated bus service gradually put the "jitneys" out of business.

## GOVERNMENT OPERATION

A unique feature of Canadian electric line development was the extent of government operation, as suggested above. In part this result was intentional, in part an accidental result of circumstances. The most extensive network of government-owned lines was that of the Canadian National. These were, with one exception, inherited by the Dominion government with the parent companies. The Canadian Northern owned three interurban systems, all acquired as a part of the vast network of Mackenzie-Mann interests. These included the Niagara, St. Catharines and Toronto, which was not physically connected with the parent company but planned as a feeder for the latter once it built to Buffalo; the Toronto Suburban, acquired by Mackenzie largely for franchise rights; and the unfinished Toronto Eastern, which was built by Mackenzie chiefly to quiet complaints of Oshawa over the bypassing of the city by the Canadian Northern's main line. Another major component of the Canadian National system, the Grand Trunk, had for many years owned one interurban, the Montreal and Southern Counties, operating in part over track of a Grand Trunk steam subsidiary, the Central Vermont. The Grand Trunk also owned the Oshawa Railway, a street car system that had an extremely important freight spur line to the General Motors plants as well as a short semi-interurban line from the lake to Ross Corners on the north edge of Oshawa.

The CNR management at first paid little attention to these lines. But after the Hydro radial schemes noted in the next chapter had failed to materialize, Sir Henry Thornton became enthusiastic about developing a series of high-speed electric railways in the Toronto–Hamilton–Niagara area. Thornton was an expansionist so far as all aspects of the CNR were concerned; rejecting the idea that the government system should content itself with a network of secondary lines rather than attempt direct competition with the CPR, he rebuilt and expanded the CNR, enlarged its hotel programme, and sought to make a super railroad out of the system. Work was resumed on the Toronto Eastern in 1923. Large sums of money were spent in modernization of the Niagara, St. Catharines and Toronto partly in conjunction with franchise renewal in St. Catharines. A 1922 offer of the city of Toronto to buy the Toronto Suburban was rejected, and a new route into Toronto was built for this line in 1925. By 1925, however, the continued growth in automobile use had made evident the folly of the general programme. Once again work was stopped on the Toronto Eastern, and the tracks were torn up, cars never having operated on them. The financially hopeless Toronto Suburban was abandoned in 1931, but the other two roads were continued because of their substantial freight business. But these were gradually allowed to deteriorate, and parts of some lines were abandoned. The Montreal and Southern Counties was finally discontinued in 1956.

The other lines owned directly or indirectly by governments included the London and Port Stanley, controlled through stock ownership by the city of London; Pictou County, acquired from the power-company owner by the Pictou County Electric Board in 1924; Nipissing Central, owned after 1911 by the Temiskaming and Northern Ontario, and thus by the Ontario government; Toronto and York Radial, acquired by the city of Toronto in 1921 and operated by Ontario Hydro from 1921 to 1924 and thence by the city (the Scarborough and Mimico lines by TTC); and the Grand Valley, owned by the city of Brantford from 1914 till abandonment, the Paris–Brantford section being operated until 1929. Both Windsor, Essex and Lake Shore and Sandwich, Windsor and Amherstburg were owned in their later years by the municipalities served. Hamilton, Grimsby and Beamsville and Brantford and Hamilton were owned for a short time prior to abandonment by Ontario Hydro, which acquired them with their power-company owner, but did not intend to continue them in operation.

Review of the experience of government operation with these lines suggests several conclusions. In the first place, government-owned lines, because of the potential tax support, could obtain funds for construction and modernization under circumstances in which private enterprise could not, or would not, do so. The ability to do so was considered an advantage to society if the project offered significant indirect benefits to the community as a whole (as for example, a subway system); otherwise, there was greater danger of waste of resources.

Secondly, government-owned lines, particularly those of the Dominion government, tended to operate for longer periods at an operating loss than did privately owned lines, partly because of political pressures to continue, partly because the losses could be borne out of tax revenue. As with construction, such conditions of operation were an advantage if there were indirect benefits to society or if the losses proved to be temporary; if not, the policy of continuing operations at a loss was uneconomic.

Finally, under the system, used in several instances, of financing entirely by bond issues, the total capital costs were less than with private enterprise, but the risk rested in full on the taxpayers, rather than upon a group of persons promoting an enterprise in the hope of high profits.

## CHAPTER FIVE

# THE PROJECTED HYDRO RADIAL SYSTEM

IN THE PERIOD between 1912 and 1922 the Ontario Hydro-Electric Power Commission, under the leadership of Sir Adam Beck, sponsored plans for a system of high-speed modern electric radial railways centring on Toronto and involving, in part, use of existing lines, in part, new construction. Beck first suggested the programme in 1912, pointing out that Hydro offered both rights of way and a source of power. He gained popular support of city councils and other groups in the area. Beck was a member of the Hearst cabinet, and in 1914 pursuaded the Ontario government to enact the basic legislation for the project, the Hydro-Electric Railway Act. The law provided that projects be initiated by the municipalities to be served and approved by the ratepayers, and that actual construction and operation would be undertaken by Ontario Hydro under contract. The projects would be financed by bonds issued by Hydro and secured by debentures issued by the municipalities, which would be responsible for covering any deficits. Beck hoped for provincial financial support in some form.

Prior to World War I, several projects were developed. The first, approved in 1914 by all but two of the municipalities involved (Uxbridge and Newmarket), consisted of a line extending north and eastward from Toronto to Markham and to Port Perry, with a branch northeastward from Markham to Uxbridge. The second, voted on in 1916 and approved by all except four jurisdictions (Berlin and three small townships), was a line to extend from Toronto via Port Credit and Guelph to London, and eventually to Sarnia. The third line, to extend from Toronto to St. Catharines and Fort Erie, was approved by all except three townships involved. Actual construction was held up by the war. Premier Hearst was at best only lukewarm in support of the plan, and had not given definite promise of a subsidy.

With the end of the war Beck renewed his efforts to get construction under way. But revision of the plans was necessitated by the fact that the Toronto Suburban had been completed to Guelph, the Toronto Eastern had been commenced, and these two and the Niagara, St. Catharines and Toronto had fallen into Dominion hands and might be available for acquisition for the system. Also, the problem of the few municipalities that had not approved the plans and the bond issues was a troublesome one, and new elections were held in an effort to obtain approval of transfer of their shares to others. In the revote, only Saltfleet refused to approve the St. Catharines line, and the municipalities on this line commenced to issue debentures and deposit them with Hydro to provide for financing. But the provincial government still would not guarantee the bonds as Beck sought, and actual construction did not get under way. In the fall elections in 1919, the plans for the radials were dealt a severe blow when the United Farmers party of E. C. Drury defeated the Hearst government. While Hearst had not been enthusiastic about the scheme, Drury was known to be very sceptical about it, and his relations with Sir Adam were not at all friendly. However, after he took office he did not condemn the plans outright, but did suggest the need for more thorough study.

Hydro then proceeded to review the plans in the light of the changed situation, and reduced the scope materially. The Port Perry project, the most unsound of all, was replaced by one for acquisition and completion of the Toronto Eastern. The London project was shelved in favour of a much more restricted Hamilton–Elmira route as well as acquisition of the Toronto Suburban and connection of it with the

FIGURE 1. The proposed Hydro radial lines as of 1913. The routes in from Markham were alternatives. (From *Canadian Railway and Marine World*, Nov. 1913, p. 540.)

Elmira line. The plans for the St. Catharines line were retained, and extended to include purchase of the Niagara, St. Catharines and Toronto. Early in 1920 the Hamilton–Elmira project was approved by voters in all municipalities served except West Flamborough, and by February all involved had approved the purchase of the

Toronto Eastern. Options were obtained by Hydro on the three electric subsidiaries of the Canadian National.

In June, Drury indicated that he would provide the guarantee once he was sure that the lines would be self supporting. But in July he held up any further action and appointed a commission, known as the Sutherland Commission for its chairman, Mr. Justice Sutherland, to investigate the proposals. The programme as reviewed by the commission consisted of five parts: (1) the Toronto Eastern, still uncompleted, which would be brought to downtown Toronto via the east Don Valley and the waterfront; (2) the Toronto, Port Credit and St. Catharines, to be built from Toronto via Port Credit, Oakville, and Hamilton to St. Catharines, either as a new road in its entirety or by making use in part of the existing lines in the area; (3) the Niagara, St. Catharines and Toronto, to be acquired and improved; (4) a line from Hamilton to Galt, Kitchener, and Elmira, and to Guelph, using in part the Grand Trunk branch lines in this area; (5) the Toronto Suburban, to be acquired and brought into downtown Toronto via Sunnyside. All lines would be built to high standards on private rights of way, with a high-speed entrance into downtown Toronto via the waterfront and a subway up Bay Street to the city hall. The lines were to be designed for both freight and passenger service. The total cost for the 326 miles was estimated at $45,644,084, or about $140,000 a mile.

The commission held extensive hearings, and in 1921 published its report, one of the most complete surveys of the intercity electric railway industry ever made.[2] The commission, much to Beck's dismay, recommended against the project, for several reasons: no new lines were being built in the United States; the financial condition of the existing lines was bad; there was no conclusive evidence that these proposed lines could support themselves. An extensive highway programme had just been undertaken, the effect of which should be considered because highway competition with the interurbans in the United States had already become serious; the new lines would in part compete with the Canadian National; the province had just borrowed heavily for the Chippawa Hydro project; guarantee of bonds for the radial lines would lead to demands for guarantee of other issues. The commission, suggested, however, that the inner portions of some of the proposed routes might have value as rapid transit facilities for the Toronto suburbs, and suggested that these be developed as a portion of the city transit system.

Sir Adam responded to the report in typical Beck fashion; he defended his proposals as the only feasible solution to the transportation problem in southern Ontario, and discounted the growth of motor vehicles. He insisted that the commission members knew nothing about the industry and chose the wrong witnesses to testify, and he stressed the difference between the high-speed lines proposed and the typical interurban in the United States.

After the adverse report, the Drury government announced that the province would not guarantee the bonds, but that the muncipalities could go ahead if they wished. They were required, however, to resubmit the proposals to the municipal councils involved, and to the voters if 15 per cent of the rate payers requested. A number of councils reapproved the Toronto–St. Catharines route, but Hamilton would not, and when the voters of Toronto disapproved the plans in an election January 1, 1923, one of the most bitterly fought in Toronto history, the project was dead. The cities then attempted to get their debentures back from Hydro, but the request was refused until certain costs relating to surveys were paid. A series of court cases ensued, and St. Catharines carried the issue to the Privy Council, only to lose.

The failure of the plans was a bitter blow to Sir Adam Beck, and, already harassed by other difficulties, particularly the claimed embezzlement of funds by his private secretary, his health broke down. When he died in 1925, the last hopes for a radial system ended.

## CHAPTER SIX

# THE STATISTICS OF THE INDUSTRY

BECAUSE THE INDUSTRY was subject to regulation and the enterprises were all corporations, data are available to a much greater extent than for most other industries.

## MILEAGE

Table V presents the data of miles built and abandoned, and miles in operation for the entire period 1887–1960, with separate figures in later years for abandonment of passenger service only. These figures have been compiled for the entire industry, from records of operations. Only intercity lines are included; street car lines owned by the same companies, and the Port Credit and Scarborough lines of Toronto and York Radial, which became essentially street car operations, have been omitted. Building dates for electrified horse-car or steam roads are those on which electric operation was established.

TABLE V

MILES OF LINE BUILT, ABANDONED, AND IN SERVICE
CANADIAN INTERCITY ELECTRIC RAILWAYS, 1887–1960

| Year | Miles built* | Miles of line abandoned† | Miles in service | Miles, passenger service discontinued† but freight service retained | Miles in passenger service‡ |
|------|------|------|------|------|------|
| 1887 | 7 | 0 | 7 | 0 | 7 |
| 1888 | 0 | 0 | 7 | 0 | 7 |
| 1889 | 2 | 0 | 9 | 0 | 9 |
| 1890 | 3 | 0 | 12 | 0 | 12 |
| 1891 | 12 | 0 | 24 | 0 | 24 |
| 1892 | 0 | 0 | 24 | 0 | 24 |
| 1893 | 22 | 0 | 46 | 0 | 46 |
| 1894 | 4 | 0 | 50 | 0 | 50 |
| 1895 | 0 | 0 | 50 | 0 | 50 |
| 1896 | 34 | 0 | 84 | 0 | 84 |
| 1897 | 30 | 0 | 114 | 0 | 114 |
| 1898 | 0 | 0 | 114 | 0 | 114 |
| 1899 | 14 | 0 | 128 | 0 | 128 |
| 1900 | 26 | 0 | 154 | 0 | 154 |
| 1901 | 27 | 0 | 181 | 0 | 181 |
| 1902 | 21 | 0 | 202 | 0 | 202 |
| 1903 | 28 | 0 | 230 | 0 | 230 |
| 1904 | 40 | 0 | 270 | 0 | 270 |
| 1905 | 43 | 5 | 308 | 0 | 308 |

SOURCE: compiled from data for individual roads.
* Mileage placed in operation during the year.
† Mileage on which service was temporarily discontinued is listed only in the year of final discontinuance.
‡ December 31 of year indicated.

TABLE V (*continued*)

| Year | Miles built* | Miles of line abandoned† | Miles in service | Miles, passenger service discontinued† but freight service retained | Miles in passenger service‡ |
|------|------|------|------|------|------|
| 1906 | 18 | 0 | 326 | 0 | 326 |
| 1907 | 77 | 0 | 403 | 0 | 403 |
| 1908 | 78 | 0 | 481 | 0 | 481 |
| 1909 | 6 | 0 | 487 | 0 | 487 |
| 1910 | 77 | 0 | 564 | 0 | 564 |
| 1911 | 23 | 0 | 587 | 0 | 587 |
| 1912 | 5 | 0 | 592 | 0 | 592 |
| 1913 | 53 | 0 | 645 | 0 | 645 |
| 1914 | 37 | 0 | 682 | 0 | 682 |
| 1915 | 31 | 0 | 713 | 0 | 713 |
| 1916 | 76 | 13 | 776 | 0 | 776 |
| 1917 | 49 | 0 | 825 | 0 | 825 |
| 1918 | 0 | 28 | 797 | 0 | 797 |
| 1919 | 0 | 0 | 797 | 0 | 797 |
| 1920 | 0 | 0 | 797 | 0 | 797 |
| 1921 | 0 | 10 | 787 | 0 | 787 |
| 1922 | 0 | 0 | 787 | 0 | 787 |
| 1923 | 0 | 7 | 780 | 0 | 780 |
| 1924 | 2 | 38 | 744 | 0 | 744 |
| 1925 | 7 | 14 | 737 | 0 | 737 |
| 1926 | 4 | 14 | 727 | 0 | 727 |
| 1927 | 0 | 14 | 713 | 41 | 672 |
| 1928 | 0 | 0 | 713 | 0 | 672 |
| 1929 | 0 | 26 | 687 | 0 | 646 |
| 1930 | 0 | 103§ | 584 | 0 | 584 |
| 1931 | 0 | 92 | 492 | 0 | 492 |
| 1932 | 0 | 48 | 444 | 0 | 444 |
| 1933 | 0 | 0 | 444 | 0 | 444 |
| 1934 | 0 | 0 | 444 | 0 | 444 |
| 1935 | 0 | 10 | 434 | 0 | 434 |
| 1936 | 0 | 0 | 434 | 0 | 434 |
| 1937 | 0 | 16 | 418 | 0 | 418 |
| 1938 | 0 | 20 | 398 | 0 | 398 |
| 1939 | 0 | 25 | 373 | 0 | 373 |
| 1940 | 0 | 0 | 373 | 0 | 373 |
| 1941 | 0 | 0 | 373 | 0 | 373 |
| 1942 | 0 | 0 | 373 | 0 | 373 |
| 1943 | 0 | 0 | 373 | 0 | 373 |
| 1944 | 0 | 0 | 373 | 0 | 373 |
| 1945 | 0 | 0 | 373 | 0 | 373 |
| 1946 | 0 | 15 | 358 | 0 | 358 |
| 1947 | 0 | 35 | 323 | 0 | 323 |
| 1948 | 0 | 14 | 309 | 0 | 309 |
| 1949 | 0 | 0 | 309 | 64 | 245 |
| 1950 | 0 | 0 | 309 | 11 | 234 |
| 1951 | 0 | 25 | 284 | 0 | 209 |
| 1952 | 0 | 0 | 284 | 7 | 202 |
| 1953 | 0 | 10 | 274 | 6 | 186 |
| 1954 | 0 | 6 | 268 | 0 | 180 |
| 1955 | 0 | 0 | 268 | 68 | 112 |
| 1956 | 0 | 26 | 242 | 10 | 76 |
| 1957 | 0 | 0 | 242 | 24 | 52 |
| 1958 | 0 | 0 | 242 | 8 | 44 |
| 1959 | 0 | 0 | 242 | 44 | 0 |

§ Including 41 miles on which passenger service had already been discontinued.

### TRAFFIC AND FINANCES

Relatively complete data on the volume of traffic and on finances were compiled by the Dominion government down until 1955; the data are far more extensive than those available in the United States. The first such statistics appeared in 1893 when an electric railway was included in the list of railways in *Railway Statistics of the Dominion of Canada*, compiled under the direction of the distinguished Chief Engineer of Railways and Canals, Collingwood Schreiber. This first line listed was the Niagara Falls Park and River; after its name appeared the notation "electric." Prior to this time the newly developed intercity electric lines were regarded as extensions of city transit systems rather than as railroads, and thus no statistics were collected. In the next five years most of the other lines in operation in this period made their appearance in the statistics volume. Commencing in the year 1901, reports were required from all electric railways, city and intercity, and the statistics were separated from those of the steam railroads, although appearing in the same volume. Forty-one companies appeared in this first tabulation, twenty-four of which were urban transit systems, including the two-mile line in Belleville, which was not destined to last out the year. In 1919, the compilation of railway and electric railway statistics was transferred to the Dominion Bureau of Statistics, and after 1922 the electric railway statistics appeared in a separate volume entitled *Statistics of Electric Railways of Canada*. The series ended with the 1955 issue.

The extent and organization of material varied somewhat over the years, to the detriment of preparation of through series in consistent fashion. Prior to 1909, the emphasis was upon physical characteristics of the lines and types of freight handled, with no reference to disposition of operating profit. From 1909 on, financial data were more complete, including the breakdown of operating expenses after the establishment in 1907 of rules relating to classification of accounts for all railroads in Canada. No further significant change occurred until 1946 when a new system of classification of accounts for transit systems and other electric railways was established, one of the major effects of which was to show net operating revenue after taxes instead of before taxes. Another was the separation of bus from rail passenger traffic and revenue. Commencing with 1920, the year-end was shifted from June 30 to December 31.

Apart from the very early years, statistics are available for all companies throughout the years of their existence, except for the little Egerton Tramways (later Pictou County) in Nova Scotia. However, for several of the companies, intercity and city operations were combined in a single enterprise, and thus separate data are not available for the intercity operations. Where the transit operations were minor, such as with the Niagara, St. Catharines and Toronto the over-all figures are employed. But with several companies the urban operations overshadowed the intercity, and it was necessary to exclude the companies from most of the tabulations. The most important of these is British Columbia Electric. The others include Cape Breton Tramways, for which separate data are available only for the periods 1904–11 and 1932–46; Hull Electric; Sandwich, Windsor and Amherstburg; and Quebec Railway. For the latter company, certain data were separated between the interurban (Montmorency) and urban (Citadel) divisions for a number of years, but complete separate data are not available. One company, Niagara Falls Park and River, has purposely been excluded from the tabulation, because it was primarily an amusement facility whose traffic volume was subject to great annual fluctuations on the basis of such

D

## TABLE VI

### Traffic and Financial Statistics of Canadian Intercity Electric Railways 1896-1955

| Year | Passengers carried — Intercity group* (000's) | Passengers carried — Intercity and suburban group† (000's) | Tons of freight — Carload group‡ (000's) | Tons of freight — LCL group§ (000's) | Number of companies in sample | Operating revenue ($000's) | Operating expenses ($000's) | Net operating income after taxes ($000's) | Operating ratio Canada | Operating ratio U.S. | Return on investment (%) Canada | Return on investment (%) U.S. |
|---|---|---|---|---|---|---|---|---|---|---|---|---|
| 1896 | — | — | — | — | 1 | 36 | 34 | 2 | 99 | — | .7 | — |
| 1897 | — | — | — | — | 1 | 36 | 23 | 13 | 63 | — | 4.6 | — |
| 1898 | — | — | — | — | 3 | 91 | 47 | 44 | 42 | — | 4.6 | — |
| 1899 | 580 | 162 | — | 4 | 3 | 96 | 49 | 47 | 51 | — | 4.5 | — |
| 1900 | 852 | 545 | 17 | 7 | 5 | 172 | 96 | 86 | 56 | — | 4.8 | 2.1 |
| 1901 | 994 | 1,940 | 74 | 6 | 7 | 304 | 192 | 127 | 63 | — | 4.2 | 2.6 |
| 1902 | 1,141 | 2,722 | 110 | 9 | 7 | 392 | 247 | 145 | 63 | — | 4.0 | 2.9 |
| 1903 | 1,215 | 3,007 | 129 | 10 | 7 | 447 | 288 | 158 | 64 | — | 4.3 | 2.7 |
| 1904 | 1,453 | 3,336 | 146 | 11 | 8 | 546 | 362 | 184 | 66 | — | 4.7 | 2.7 |
| 1905 | 1,924 | 4,389 | 168 | 9 | 8 | 651 | 425 | 226 | 67 | — | 5.6 | 2.9 |
| 1906 | 1,976 | 4,695 | 192 | 23 | 8 | 753 | 489 | 264 | 65 | — | 5.9 | 2.7 |
| 1907 | 2,142 | 5,204 | 207 | 42 | 9 | 890 | 601 | 289 | 68 | 59 | 5.6 | 2.8 |
| 1908 | 2,808 | 5,666 | 250 | 42 | 11 | 1,097 | 786 | 294 | 73 | 60 | 3.9 | 2.8 |
| 1909 | 3,444 | 7,349 | 276 | 66 | 12 | 1,365 | 867 | 405 | 64 | 59 | 4.3 | 2.8 |
| 1910 | 4,130 | 8,037 | 409 | 90 | 13 | 1,593 | 1,093 | 525 | 65 | 58 | 5.5 | 3.1 |
| 1911 | 5,854 | 10,388 | 512 | 117 | 15 | 2,058 | 1,325 | 700 | 64 | 59 | 6.1 | 3.2 |
| 1912 | 7,033 | 11,596 | 741 | 178 | 15 | 2,327 | 1,550 | 734 | 67 | 63 | 5.2 | 3.1 |
| 1913 | 7,872 | 13,943 | 1,134 | 185 | 15 | 2,704 | 1,744 | 884 | 66 | 63 | 6.3 | 3.2 |
| 1914 | 8,331 | 16,246 | 1,012 | 176 | 15 | 3,028 | 2,213 | 829 | 72 | 68 | 5.4 | 2.8 |
| 1915 | 7,695 | 16,407 | 912 | 154 | 15 | 2,948 | 2,179 | 730 | 75 | 67 | 4.6 | 2.7 |
| 1916 | 8,363 | 17,632 | 1,275 | 159 | 17 | 3,298 | 2,314 | 899 | 70 | 67 | 5.2 | 2.8 |
| 1917 | 8,570 | 19,182 | 1,534 | 167 | 17 | 3,673 | 2,765 | 899 | 75 | 76 | 4.0 | 3.0 |
| 1918 | 8,367 | 21,205 | 1,749 | 174 | 16 | 4,022 | 3,109 | 829 | 77 | 75 | 3.5 | 2.7 |
| 1919 | 8,327 | 22,200 | 1,457 | 172 | 16 | 4,733 | 3,745 | 909 | 79 | 76 | 4.3 | 3.0 |
| 1920 | 9,196 | 28,921 | 1,647 | 239 | 16 | 5,986 | 5,201 | 688 | 87 | 79 | 3.2 | 3.0 |
| 1921 | 9,261 | 28,730 | 1,464 | 230 | 16 | 6,038 | 5,298 | 639 | 88 | 84 | 3.0 | 2.1 |
| 1922 | 8,701 | 26,728 | 1,325 | 295 | 16 | 5,640 | 4,897 | 617 | 87 | 81 | 2.9 | 2.3 |
| 1923 | 8,544 | 20,449 | 1,769 | 366 | 16 | 5,431 | 4,852 | 461 | 89 | 83 | 2.0 | 2.3 |
| 1924 | 7,814 | 18,194 | 1,448 | 247 | 15 | 4,877 | 4,704 | 184 | 97 | 85 | 1.4 | 2.2 |
| 1925 | 7,037 | 17,893 | 1,459 | 230 | 14 | 4,817 | 4,612 | 70 | 96 | 87 | .3 | 1.8 |
| 1926 | 6,717 | 15,448 | 1,998 | 257 | 14 | 5,010 | 4,474 | 386 | 89 | 91 | 1.6 | 1.1 |
| 1927 | 6,334 | 15,669 | 1,798 | 258 | 14 | 4,775 | 4,370 | 250 | 92 | 91 | 1.0 | 1.1 |
| 1928 | 5,812 | 15,732 | 2,358 | 227 | 14 | 4,839 | 4,373 | 328 | 90 | 90 | 1.3 | .9 |
| 1929 | 5,316 | 11,109 | 2,338 | 175 | 13 | 4,391 | 3,747 | 489 | 86 | 93 | -1.9 | .5 |

**TABLE VI** (*continued*)

| Year | Passengers carried Inter-city group* (000's) | Passengers carried Intercity and suburban group† (000's) | Tons of freight Carload group‡ (000's) | Tons of freight LCL group§ (000's) | Number of companies in sample | Operating revenue ($000's) | Operating expenses ($000's) | Net operating income after taxes ($000's) | Operating ratio Canada | Operating ratio U.S. | Return on investment (%) Canada | Return on investment (%) U.S. |
|---|---|---|---|---|---|---|---|---|---|---|---|---|
| 1930 | 4,159 | 8,615 | 1,849 | 166 | 12 | 3,386 | 3,106 | 171 | 92 | 101 | .7 | −.5 |
| 1931 | 3,878 | 6,900 | 1,284 | 100 | 10 | 2,361 | 2,428 | −185 | 103 | 101 | −.8 | −.9 |
| 1932 | 2,902 | 5,495 | 1,002 | 27 | 8 | 1,760 | 1,970 | −346 | 112 | 115 | −1.2 | −1.3 |
| 1933 | 2,201 | 4,933 | 1,023 | 7 | 6 | 1,524 | 1,593 | −162 | 105 | 110 | −.6 | −.8 |
| 1934 | 2,169 | 4,125 | 1,253 | 6 | 6 | 1,605 | 1,584 | −106 | 99 | 106 | −.7 | −.6 |
| 1935 | 1,918 | 4,044 | 1,364 | 7 | 6 | 1,651 | 1,638 | −76 | 99 | 104 | −.5 | −.3 |
| 1936 | 1,995 | 4,186 | 1,477 | 6 | 6 | 1,708 | 1,667 | −47 | 98 | 100 | −.3 | 0 |
| 1937 | 1,981 | 4,584 | 1,658 | 8 | 6 | 1,778 | 1,637 | 52 | 92 | 105 | −.3 | −.6 |
| 1938 | 1,970 | 5,255 | 1,407 | 7 | 6 | 1,629 | 1,669 | −120 | 102 | 105 | −.8 | −.7 |
| 1939 | 1,999 | 5,164 | 1,547 | 7 | 6 | 1,708 | 1,698 | −75 | 99 | 101 | −.6 | −.1 |
| 1940 | 1,446 | 4,353 | 1,612 | 0 | 5 | 1,863 | 1,922 | −140 | 103 | 100 | −2.0 | 0 |
| 1941 | 1,855 | 5,916 | 1,999 | 0 | 5 | 2,375 | 2,121 | 106 | 91 | 97 | .8 | .6 |
| 1942 | 2,529 | 7,580 | 2,325 | 0 | 5 | 2,931 | 2,450 | 384 | 84 | 87 | 2.8 | 3.1 |
| 1943 | 3,329 | 10,088 | 2,395 | 0 | 5 | 3,463 | 2,818 | 490 | 81 | 88 | 3.6 | 3.0 |
| 1944 | 3,291 | 10,723 | 2,343 | 0 | 5 | 3,558 | 3,246 | 212 | 91 | 87 | 1.5 | 3.7 |
| 1945 | 2,872 | 11,146 | 2,320 | 0 | 5 | 3,615 | 3,296 | 212 | 91 | 89 | 1.5 | 3.5 |
| 1946 | 2,608 | 10,919 | 2,349 | 0 | 5 | 3,573 | 3,561 | −107 | 100 | 96 | −.8 | 1.1 |
| 1947 | 1,962 | 9,466 | 2,454 | 0 | 5 | 3,656 | 3,888 | −310 | 106 | 99 | −2.3 | .3 |
| 1948 | 1,781 | 6,249 | 2,806 | 0 | 5 | 3,931 | 4,925 | −1,163 | 125 | — | −9.0 | — |
| 1949 | 1,469 | 5,341 | 2,615 | 0 | 5 | 3,936 | 4,438 | −680 | 113 | — | −5.4 | — |
| 1950 | 1,214 | 4,237 | 2,857 | 0 | 5 | 4,033 | 4,533 | −686 | 113 | — | −5.6 | — |
| 1951 | 886 | 4,078 | 3,119 | 0 | 5 | 4,399 | 4,796 | −619 | 109 | — | −5.4 | — |
| 1952 | 608 | 3,956 | 2,897 | 0 | 5 | 4,356 | 4,472 | −328 | 103 | — | −2.9 | — |
| 1953 | 476 | 3,927 | 2,755 | 0 | 5 | 4,389 | 4,784 | −604 | 109 | — | −5.3 | — |
| 1954 | 368 | 3,670 | 2,637 | 0 | 5 | 3,868 | 4,515 | −650 | 117 | — | −7.8 | — |
| 1955 | 215 | 2,120 | 3,000 | 0 | 5 | 3,593 | 4,792 | −1,334 | 133 | — | −9.3 | — |

SOURCE: Canada, Dominion Bureau of Statistics, *Statistics of Electric Railways* (Ottawa, various years); G. W. Hilton and J. F. Due, *The Electric Interurban Railways in America* (Stanford, 1960), pp. 186-87.

* Includes Chatham, Wallaceburg and Lake Erie; Brantford and Hamilton; Windsor, Essex and Lake Shore; Nipissing Central; Grand River; Lake Erie and Northern; South Western; London and Port Stanley; Hamilton, Grimsby, and Beamsville; Hamilton Radial; Winnipeg, Selkirk and Lake Winnipeg.

† Includes Montreal and Southern Counties; Hamilton and Dundas; Toronto and York Radial; Toronto Suburban; Niagara, St. Catharines and Toronto.

‡ Includes British Columbia Electric; Chatham, Wallaceburg and Lake Erie; Grand River; Lake Erie and Northern; London and Port Stanley; Niagara, St. Catharines and Toronto.

§ Includes Toronto and Hamilton area lines; Winnipeg, Selkirk and Lake Winnipeg; South Western; and Windsor lines.

factors as weather and organization of excursions by steam railroads. Accordingly, its inclusion would tend to distort the typical trends in the industry.

*Passenger Traffic*

Figure 2 shows the trends in passenger traffic over the life of the industry. The companies have been divided into two classes, those with primarily intercity operation, such as the Brantford and Hamilton, and those which handled a large volume of short distance suburban commuter traffic, namely, Montreal and Southern Counties, Toronto and York Radial, Toronto Suburban, and the Hamilton and Dundas,

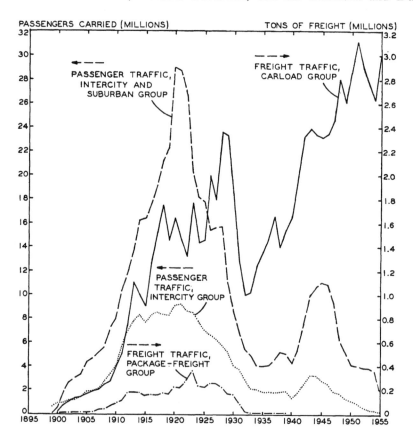

FIGURE 2. Passenger and freight traffic, intercity electric railways, 1898–1955. (Source: Canada, Dominion Bureau of Statistics, *Statistics of Electric Railways* (Ottawa, various years.)
Intercity group includes Chatham, Wallaceburg and Lake Erie; Brantford and Hamilton; Windsor, Essex and Lake Shore; Nipissing Central; Grand River; Lake Erie and Northern, South Western; London and Port Stanley; Hamilton, Grimbsy and Beamsville; Hamilton Radial; Winnipeg, Selkirk and Lake Winnipeg.
Intercity and suburban group includes Montreal and Southern Counties; Hamilton and Dundas; Toronto and York Radial; Toronto Surbuban; Niagara, St. Catharines and Toronto.
Carload group includes British Columbia Electric; Chatham, Wallaceburg and Lake Erie; Grand River; Lake Erie and Northern; London and Port Stanley; Niagara, St. Catharines and Toronto.
Package-freight (LCL) group includes Toronto and Hamilton area lines; Winnipeg, Selkirk and Lake Winnipeg; South Western; Windsor lines.

or which carried substantial urban traffic, including the Niagara, St. Catharines and Toronto, and Toronto Suburban.

Up to 1912, the rate of growth of the two groups was similar. But in the next eight years the volume of the intercity-suburban group increased tremendously, while that of the other had more or less stabilized. However, the peak year for the latter was 1921, for the former 1920. The path of the decline was similar for the two groups. One suburban line, Montreal and Southern Counties, did not reach its all-time high until 1946. In contrast, four of the intercity operations reached their peaks in the 1913–15 period, the others in the 1920–23 period. One intercity company, the London and Port Stanley, reached an all-time high in 1943 when volume was five times that of 1934.

The growth in volume in the earlier years reflects in part, of course, the increasing number of companies. But in general, with isolated exceptions, the traffic volume of each line grew substantially up until 1914. Almost all lines experienced a drop in 1915; a few lost business continuously from this year on, but most recovered gradually to peaks in the early twenties. From then on the drop was continuous through the twenties as automobile use expanded rapidly. By 1929 most companies had little more than half the peak-year volume. The Chatham, Wallaceburg and Lake Erie experienced the worst drop, its 1926 volume being scarcely 20 per cent of the 1914 peak. Montreal and Southern Counties, with its growing suburban traffic, was the last to reach its pre-World War II peak (1924), and its 1929 traffic was only slightly less. The depression brought an end to many operations, and drastic losses in traffic to the remainder. For most of those which survived, traffic increased slightly as recovery came, and then very sharply during the war to bring the volume for the five remaining companies for which data are available back close to or in excess of the original peaks. Then came another drastic decline. By 1954, the Lake Erie and Northern, the Grand River, and the London and Port Stanley had only about 10 per cent of their 1944 figures and far less than their depression lows.

*Freight Traffic*

Although the typical early electric railroad was designed to be a passenger carrier, and freight service was limited to package freight carried on the interurban cars or special freight cars equipped with motors, there were three early exceptions. The Niagara, St. Catharines and Toronto, originally a steam road handling regular freight traffic, had a substantial volume from the time of electrification, and prior to 1905 carried more tonnage than all other electrified intercity lines together. But it was soon rivalled by the Grand River, which the Canadian Pacific developed into a freight feeder line in the area north of Galt that was not served directly by the parent road. British Columbia Electric, which leased the Vancouver and Lulu Island from the CPR, entered the carload freight business at an early date, but this was largely switching and terminal work until the Fraser Valley line was built. The other important early freight carrier was the Hamilton, Grimsby and Beamsville, which, despite its street-car-like track running on the edge of the road, soon established a considerable volume of traffic in fruit from the Niagara Peninsula to Hamilton.

After 1910 the total freight traffic became much more important, as several of the new lines were designed to handle carload traffic. This was true of the Chatham, Wallaceburg and Lake Erie, the Lake Erie and Northern, initially planned as a steam and primarily freight-traffic road, and the London and Port Stanley, an electrified steam road. Other roads, such as the Windsor, Essex and Lake Shore, had some freight traffic. One group, however, never succeeded in developing this service beyond a small amount of package freight—Hamilton Radial (which also did limited carload switching in Hamilton), the Brantford and Hamilton, the Cape Breton, the Grand Valley, the Woodstock, Thames Valley and Ingersoll, and the London and Lake Erie. In a few instances freight was handled on the same track by another company, as, for example, by the Toronto, Hamilton and Buffalo on the Hamilton and Dundas.

Two other electric railways in Canada developed very important carload freight traffic, even though they did not operate intercity lines and thus are not included in this study. One is Oshawa Railway, a subsidiary of the Grand Trunk and subsequently of Canadian National, which serves the General Motors plants and other industries, and the Cornwall Street Railway Light and Power Company, which provides facilities for a number of industries in that city. Both have ceased to operate street car service. By 1955 the Oshawa line had greater freight revenue than any Canadian electric line except British Columbia Electric and the Grand River–Lake Erie and Northern, and the Cornwall had greater tonnage than any electric roads other than these.

Of the larger roads, the two Canadian Pacific subsidiaries consistently showed the greatest percentage of freight revenue to total. The Grand River was gaining 50 per cent from freight by 1910 and 65 per cent by 1930 and the Lake Erie and Northern about 30 per cent at first, 40 per cent by 1923, and 50 per cent by 1927. The combined figures for these two roads were 70 per cent for a number of years, and had climbed to 90 per cent by 1950. The Chatham, Wallaceburg and Lake Erie likewise showed a 40 per cent figure by 1911, 50 per cent by 1918, and 90 per cent by 1926. Unfortunately, percentages alone cannot make a road profitable; the absolute volume was not adequate to allow profits to be earned. The London and Port Stanley showed freight traffic of 40 to 50 per cent for many years, but as passenger traffic declined the percentage rose to 60 by 1955. The Niagara–St. Catharines road, with a substantial volume of urban passenger revenue, gained 30 per cent from freight for years; the figure rose to 50 per cent in the late twenties, declined during World War II, and then rose again. The Hamilton, Grimsby and Beamsville gained from 20 to 30 per cent during most of its life, the figure falling to 10 per cent in the last few years before abandonment.

Figure 2 shows the trends in freight traffic over the years. Ton-mileage figures are not available, and therefore tons handled must be used instead. The roads are grouped into two classes, six roads that developed extensive carload traffic (British Columbia Electric, the Chatham–Wallaceburg line, the two Canadian Pacific subsidiaries, the London and Port Stanley, and the Niagara, St. Catharines and Toronto), and nine others whose freight traffic consisted primarily of LCL (less than carload) package freight. The difference in the behaviour of traffic of the two groups is phenomenal. The LCL group reached its maximum in 1923, and by 1929 the volume had fallen in half (to a figure less than in 1913). The traffic was almost nil (and most of these roads were abandoned) by 1933. The carload group continued to rise steadily through the twenties, the pre-depression peak (1928) being 50 per cent greater than the 1918 figure. The volume fell in half in the depression, but returned to old levels in World War II, and reached its all-time peak in 1951. The 1955 figure, the last for which information was available, was the second highest year. The greatest gainers in the post-war period were British Columbia Electric and the Grand River lines; the former's peak year was 1955. The London and Port Stanley reached its peak in 1929, the 1955 figure being scarcely half as great, and the Niagara line's peak year was 1937.

*Finances*

Figure 3 gives an over-all summary of the financial history of the industry from its earliest years down to 1955. The upper portion of the graph shows the trends in total operating revenues, total operating expenses, and operating profit after taxes. Operating profit before taxes figures cannot be compiled for the entire period; furthermore, taxes comprised only a small fraction of expenses, and were primarily real property taxes and thus in a sense payments for local government services. The centre portion of the graph shows the behaviour of the operating ratio, and the lower portion the

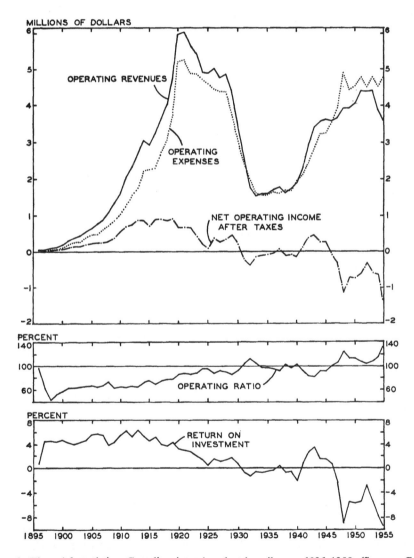

FIGURE 3. Financial statistics, Canadian intercity electric railways, 1896–1955. (Source: Canada, Dominion Bureau of Statistics, *Statistics of Electric Railways* (Ottawa, various years.)

return on investment. The latter involves some estimation, because the investment figures reported in the accounts of the firms were in general greatly exaggerated, except for a few roads built at a relatively late date when accounts were subject to supervision. The earlier roads were financed almost entirely by sale of bonds, the stock representing little or no investment of money. The value of road and equipment was then written up to approximate the sum of the heavily watered capitalization. Some roads cost even less than the sum of the bonds issued because the latter were sold at a discount. For this study, the investment figures were estimated on the basis of typical cost-of-track and equipment data per mile for the various periods, plus such other data as were available. These figures must be regarded merely as estimates, but they are probably substantially more correct than the reported figures. Although entirely accurate adjustments for write-offs and for new equipment and improvements could not be made, the measure of the rate of return gives a relatively satisfactory measure of trends in earnings over the years.

The major features of the trends can be summarized. Operating revenues grew steadily from 1896 down through 1921, the 1921 figure being twice that of 1914 (part of the increase reflecting price level change). Only in the year 1915 did a drop in revenue occur (and then only slightly) in this entire period. Part of the increase in earlier years, of course reflected additional mileage. Operating expenses grew at a slightly faster pace, and thus, although net operating income increased in dollar terms, the operating ratio rose steadily, from 42 per cent in 1898 and 56 in 1900 to from 60 to 69 per cent in the 1901–13 period and over 70 after 1916. The rise in total volume offset the increasing operating ratio up to 1913, and in that year the rate of return reached its maximum, 6.3 per cent. From 1897 to 1913 the figure fluctuated in the relatively narrow range from 3.9 to 6.3, with a gradual rise except for two relatively bad years, 1908 and 1909, when the industry suffered from the general business depression. It is interesting to note that the growth in automobile usage had not caused sufficient inroads on business to prevent total traffic from increasing up to 1921.

From 1921 to 1929, despite general prosperity in the economy, gross revenue fell steadily to $4.4 million in 1929 against $6.0 million in 1922; the effect of the automobile was now obvious. The roads were surprisingly successful in cutting operating expenses (in part a reflection of abandonment of some lines), but nevertheless the operating ratio rose; the high for the period was 97 per cent (1924) before some of the worst roads were abandoned. The rate of return, which had commenced to drop in 1914 and by 1921 was only half of the 1914 figure, continued to decline, although with some irregularity; the low for the decade was .3 per cent in 1925, and the 1929 figure was 1.9.

The depression came just at the time that the industry was already weakened by automobile competition, and caused a drastic loss in traffic and destruction of the weak roads. Revenues fell from $4.4 million in 1929 to a low of $1.5 million in 1933, one-fourth of the 1921 high. Of the sixteen companies in the group for 1921, only six were left by 1933. Except for 1937, the companies as a whole showed a deficit from 1931 to 1939; recovery of the economy brought only a slight improvement, although gross revenue increased somewhat, to $1.7 million in 1939.

The war, of course, brought sharp increases in traffic as production increased and motor vehicle use was restricted, and by 1945 total revenues had risen to $3.6 million. Of the six companies in the sample still operating in 1933, only one, the Winnipeg–Selkirk line, was abandoned down to the time that the series ended in 1955. During the war years, the rate of return reached a high of 3.6 per cent in 1943. In the post-war years, revenues continued to rise to a high of $4.4 million in 1951 as freight revenue rose; thereafter they declined to $3.6 million in 1955, mainly because passenger traffic fell drastically. But expenses grew still more rapidly; most of the increase in revenues merely reflected price level changes, not greater volume, and wage and materials costs tended to outstrip these revenues. The five roads as a group showed a deficit in every year from 1946 through 1955; in 1955 the operating ratio was 133 per cent and the return on investment a negative 9.3 per cent.

On the whole, the rate of return over the years of the industry was not sufficient to attract capital into the industry. The highest figure, 6.3 per cent in 1913, was barely adequate in terms of usual standards, and the typical figure in the developmental years, from 4 to 5 per cent, was clearly inadequate. Figures of return on reported investment indicate an even lower rate of return, as shown in Table VII by the figures for selected years.

TABLE VII

COMPARISON OF RATES OF RETURN ON ESTIMATED INVESTMENT AND ON
REPORTED CAPITAL, SELECTED YEARS 1909–1924

| Year | Rate of return on (percentage) | |
|---|---|---|
| | Estimated capital investment | Reported total capital investment |
| 1909 | 4.3 | 2.8 |
| 1914 | 5.4 | 3.9 |
| 1919 | 4.3 | 3.7 |
| 1924 | 1.4 | .8 |

The expansion of the industry was based primarily on the expectation of improvements in the future, improvements that would have come had the population continued to increase and the automobile not developed. But when the upward trend did not continue after 1913, expansion came to an abrupt end. Sir Adam Beck's optimism in promoting the radial system in subsequent years can be explained only in terms of his belief that the high-speed lines which he proposed could be more successful financially than the existing roads—a belief that would likely have been realized to only a limited degree. Sir Adam was also a strong adherent of the "auto is a fad" doctrine that was popular in this period in the United States; he apparently felt that car use would fall once people became tired of the novelty.

Table VIII gives some indication of the number of years that firms operated at an operating loss, both immediately prior to abandonment and during their entire history. The record of Montreal and Southern Counties is little short of phenomenal. Prior to its abandonment in 1956, the line operated for twenty-five consecutive years at an operating loss, even on a before-tax basis. The accumulated sum of operating losses (including taxes) over this period was $5 million. In later years the gross revenues were less than half the operating expenses. In part, however, the losses reflected what appear to have been unreasonable charges by the CNR for use of the Victoria Bridge. Niagara Falls Park and River showed losses for eleven years, but it was a portion of an integrated system, and contributed to the business of the parent International Railway. Toronto Suburban showed nine years of losses; Hamilton

TABLE VIII

Operating Loss Record of Canadian Intercity Electric Railways
(20 companies)

| Years of operation at operating loss | Over life of company | Number of companies | | | |
|---|---|---|---|---|---|
| | | | Immediately before abandonment | | |
| | | Private | Municipal-provincial | Dominion | Total* |
| 0 | 1 | 4 | | | 4 |
| 1–2 | 3 | 4 | | | 4 |
| 3–6 | 5 | 1 | | | 1 |
| 7–9 | 5 | 1 | 3 | 1 | 5 |
| 10–15 | 5 | 1 | | | 1 |
| 16–25 | 0 | | | 1 | 1 |
| 26–31 | 1 | | | | |

*Four of the companies included are still in operation.

Radial, Toronto and York Radial, and Windsor, Essex and Lake Shore eight years (partly under private, partly under public ownership). On the other hand, four discontinued without showing a loss the preceding year, and two of these never showed a loss (before taxes)—Winnipeg, Selkirk and Lake Winnipeg, and, oddly, Woodstock, Thames Valley and Ingersoll, which for most of its life barely covered operating expenses yet never fell into the red.

Table VIII also shows the number of years of operation at a loss immediately before abandonment, classified by ownership—private, municipal-provincial, and Dominion. One very obvious conclusion appears: privately operated roads are much less likely to run at a deficit for any length of time than government roads, especially if Dominion owned. Governments have the resources to meet deficits; they are not under the same pressure to liquidate while funds are left for the creditors; and they are subject to political pressures to keep the enterprises in operation. As would be expected, the Dominion government is more subject to these influences than local governments. Such a policy on the part of the federal government may be regarded as justifiable if there are important secondary benefits from the activities to the community as a whole, such as the lessening of traffic congestion. But examination of the electric lines that were operated at losses for long periods shows little evidence that there were such secondary benefits of any magnitude or that these influenced the action. Nor were the worst offenders—Montreal and Southern Counties and Toronto Suburban—making any significant contribution to the traffic of the parent Canadian National system, as was true of the Niagara, St. Catharines and Toronto. With both of these roads there appears to be no explanation beyond local pressures to keep the roads going, and inertia on the part of the parent system. Yet the deficits were not negligible; the $500,000 deficit the Montreal line was running for several years was a significant element in the CNR total net earnings or loss picture in these years.

The median length of life of the enterprises was 34 years, with five over 50 years, four from 40 to 49, seven from 30 to 39, seven from 20 to 29, and two under 20. The shortest life of any enterprise was the 11 years of the London and Lake Erie, and the Grand Valley did little better with 14 years (a portion of the track was operated by the city of Brantford for a longer period). By contrast, British Columbia Electric had been in operation 74 years as of 1964; the Niagara, St. Catharines and Toronto, including its predecessor lines, had been in operation 77 years as an electric line at the end of 1964, and the Grand River had reached 70 years. All of these had ceased to operate passenger service. London and Port Stanley completed 48 years of electric operation in 1964, but had been in existence as a railroad for 109 years.

STRONG VERSUS WEAK ROADS. Inevitably, the roads varied substantially in their ability to cover costs and earn an adequate return on investment. None of the roads, of course, earned a normal return over their entire lives; those roads which continued to operate beyond the early thirties were able to continue only through the aid of their railroad owners, except for the London and Port Stanley, which was able to cover operating expenses. If the period prior to 1930 is considered, however, several of the lines consistently earned an adequate return on estimated actual investment and even in some years on the reported investment figures. The most consistently profitably road was the Grand River, which in the thirty-two years prior to 1931 (when its accounts were consolidated with those of the Lake Erie and Northern) earned a return better than 5 per cent in twenty-five years, and in nine of these years the figure exceeded 10 per cent. This line served a heavily populated industrial area, developed substantial carload freight, and because of its early date of construction enjoyed a relatively low investment figure. The London and Port Stanley, despite all that has been said in London about its white-elephant characteristics, did well after electrification in 1915, earning from 5 to 8 per cent consistently through 1929, and suffering deficits in only six of the forty years of its history as an electric road, down through 1955. Toronto and York Radial consistently earned 7 to 10 per cent through 1922; in twenty-one of its first twenty-two years it earned over 5 per cent and in eight of these, more than 10 per cent. After 1922 it collapsed, suffering deficits in the remaining eight years of its life. The Hamilton Grimsby, and Beamsville, with a very low investment per mile, did extremely well from 1899 through 1915, averaging from 8 to 18 per cent, but did very poorly after 1916.

Another group of roads slowly improved their earnings from the lean early years, enjoyed a few years of adequate return, and then lapsed into deficits. This group included such lines as Nipissing Central, the Niagara, St. Catharines and Toronto, the Brantford and Hamilton (whose best years came after 1918, when some roads were on the downgrade), the Chatham, Wallaceburg and Lake Erie, whose collapse started early (1917), and the Windsor, Essex and Lake Shore (which remained profitable through 1923 and then rapidly declined). The Hamilton and Dundas was somewhat unique in earning a consistent but barely adequate return of from 4 to 6 per cent through its history prior to 1919, when it lapsed into deficits. South Western Traction had a moderate return consistently down through 1915, when it was destroyed by the electrification of the London and Port Stanley.

At the other extreme, a few lines were spectacularly unsuccessful. Toronto Suburban was one of the few lines to be relatively unprofitable in its early years; as the population of the area it served grew, it attained a few years of successful operation around 1910. But once it built its extension to Guelph the rate of return fell sharply and deficits were incurred annually after 1923. The Grand Valley and its affiliate the Woodstock, Thames Valley and Ingersoll earned as much as 5 per cent in only one year (1903); otherwise the return was typically from 1 to 2 per cent, and deficits were avoided only by holding down operating expenses to minimum levels. Although the road, strangely, never showed an actual deficit, the income was too low to allow even adequate maintenance expenditures, and by 1912 the Grand Valley itself was barely able to keep its cars on the track. Hamilton Radial was able to earn an adequate if not large return prior to 1906 and in some of the following years, but after 1914 the returns were extremely low, and deficits were frequent after 1918. The Winnipeg, Selkirk and Lake Winnipeg was in a sense unique because, although it never earned as much as 5 per cent and rarely over 3, it never incurred a deficit except in the three worst years of the depression, and it lasted until 1939.

The record for the longest period of unprofitable operation belonged to the Montreal and Southern Counties. As a suburban carrier it earned a moderate return in 1912 and 1913, then suffered deficits when it extended its interurban line, but enjoyed roughly a 5 per cent return in the twenties down through 1930, a period when many roads were losing traffic sharply. In 1931 a deficit appeared and continued for the next twenty-five years as noted above.

The tables on finances do not include British Columbia Electric, because of the impossibility of separating urban and intercity line finances. Without much question this operation was more profitable than the average line, and the traffic held up better than many roads, partly because of the rapid population growth. Passenger service was operated on the Central Park line to New Westminster for sixty-three years, a length of time exceeded by only one line in the United States (Portland–Oregon City).

DIVIDEND RECORD. The figures of dividend payments are not entirely satisfactory because no over-all figures are available for the years prior to 1909, and for several of the larger systems no breakdown is possible between the interurban and urban line earnings and dividends. But figures for some nineteen companies are available from 1909 on, although not all of the companies were in operation for all of the years. Between the years 1909 and 1920 inclusive, no more than two companies paid dividends in any one year; the total amount of annual dividends varied between $12,000 and $31,000, in the peak year of 1912. These figures are of course phenomenally low. Most of the systems never paid a dividend in the entire period. Payments were made by the Grand River ($12,500 in the years 1915–20), Egerton Tramways (two years), the Hamilton and Dundas (six years), the Hamilton, Grimsby and Beamsville (three years). From 1921 through 1937 no dividends were paid by any of the lines.

## CHAPTER SEVEN

# THE DECLINE

THE DATA OF the preceding chapter suggest the fate of the industry, but a more careful review of the decline is warranted. It is difficult to mark the exact turning point. The peak of expansion came in the 1907–10 period, although there was substantial construction thereafter. In a sense 1913 may be regarded as the peak year, as the rate of return reached its high in that year. The year 1916 was the last one in which any significant construction occurred, the forty-nine miles that Toronto Suburban placed in service in 1917 having been built largely in earlier years. On the other hand passenger volume for the roads as a whole and gross revenue continued to rise through 1921, although some roads experienced declines as early as 1914. Thus the 1913–22 period marked the end of expansion in the industry. At first however, there was little thought that decline had set in. For example, it was during this period that Sir Adam Beck was pushing his radial plans, and as late as 1923 the Canadian National Railways, in the general spirit of enthusiasm and expansion which marked its early years under Sir Henry Thornton, commenced to complete the Toronto Eastern (Toronto–Oshawa–Bowmanville), and spent substantial sums modernizing the Niagara–St. Catharines road.

The cessation of new construction can be attributed to two factors: the failure of the rate of return in the industry to increase as expected and to attain levels sufficient to attract new capital, and the realization that the motor vehicle was going to have some effect on traffic. Although the potential of the automobile was not adequately recognized during the 1913–22 period, some consideration was inevitably given to it, particularly after 1920, as shown by testimony to the Sutherland Commission investigating the Hydro radial plans. And in 1924 the trend downward was well enough marked that the CNR, which along with Sir Adam Beck was among the last to recognize the significance of the automobile, suddenly abandoned the Toronto Eastern project. Also, the absorption of the Grand Trunk Railway into the Canadian National system in 1923 provided one other shore route through Oshawa, and there was little need for another

The actual decline in rate of return was relatively gradual during the twenties, as shown by the charts in the previous chapter, in part because carload freight traffic was rising. But the decline was more or less universal, and by 1929 the number of passengers had fallen 40 per cent and the rate of return to less than 2 per cent. The weaker roads inevitably were the first to experience operating deficits, and to face complete abandonment. Prior to 1921 there had been only three abandonments, all of which resulted from special circumstances. The first, which occurred in 1905, was the Hamilton, Grimsby and Beamsville's extension to Vineland, after one year of operating losses, and the decision of the Niagara, St. Catherines and Toronto not to build the connecting link to St. Catharines. In 1916 the Grand Valley, which had long been plagued by inadequate traffic and had let its line deteriorate to the point at which operations were unsafe, was abandoned as soon as the parallel Lake Erie and Northern line was completed. And in 1918 the once profitable London and Lake Erie was forced out of operation by the electrification of the parallel London and

Port Stanley. Subsequent abandonments did not occur until the twenties, and even then the movement began slowly with the Hamilton and Dundas in 1923, the Saanich line of British Columbia Electric in 1924, and Hamilton Radial's Oakville line, along with Woodstock, Thames Valley and Ingersoll, in 1925. In 1927 the Chatham, Wallaceburg and Lake Erie discontinued passenger service, and the Schomberg line of Toronto and York Radial was abandoned. In 1929 the rest of Hamilton Radial came out. These were for the most part weak roads with limited traffic potentialities and more vulnerable to motor competition, but by 1929 a number of other roads were in very precarious condition. Pictou County was abandoned early in 1930.

The depression struck very hard at the already weakened industry, causing sharp declines in traffic even on the best lines, particularly in freight traffic, which for the lines specializing in carload traffic had thus far been little affected by trucking. From 1930 to 1932 inclusive 250 miles were abandoned, including some of the previously strong roads. The abandonment of Toronto and York Radial's main line in 1930 came as a great shock to many. The Chatham line also discontinued all operations. The following year saw the end of the two remaining Hamilton lines, the relatively new but hopelessly unprofitable line of Toronto Suburban, and the Niagara-on-the-Lake line. In 1932 the recently rebuilt Windsor, Essex and Lake Shore and the Niagara Falls Park and River ceased operations.

In the period from 1925 to 1931 the attitude of the management towards the decline varied considerably. Some lines made little or no effort to fight the downward trend, operating along the same patterns until abandonment, which they apparently foresaw some years in advance. This was the case with all of the Hamilton lines, for example. Some entered the bus business, as previously noted, to protect themselves, but the general unprofitability of bus operation in the period did not encourage this policy. There was much less over-all modernization than in the United States. The most complete was that of the Windsor, Essex and Lake Shore, which under municipal ownership was rebuilt and re-equipped in 1929 and 1930, only to be abandoned two years later. In this instance, the declining revenues had been attributed almost entirely to the failure to modernize, when actually they were in large measure the reflection of a trend that modernization could not check. The Niagara, St. Catharines and Toronto was also rebuilt and modernized during the mid-twenties, with less unhappy results than those of the Windsor, Essex and Lake Shore.

Several other smaller lines struggled on for a few years in the hope that recovery of business activity would restore profits. The province-owned Nipissing Central lasted until 1935, the Sandwich, Windsor and Amherstburg until 1938, and the Winnipeg, Selkirk and Lake Winnipeg until 1937 (Selkirk) and 1939 (Stonewall). With World War II business for the remaining lines tended to rise because of increased employment and shortages of gasoline and new automobiles, and no mileage was abandoned over this period. At this time there remained largely intact the three lines in Quebec, the Niagara, St. Catharines and Toronto, the CPR lines in the Grand Valley, the London and Port Stanley, British Columbia Electric, and the little line on Cape Breton. Most of these relied heavily on carload freight traffic, but all provided frequent passenger service. The lines operated 373 miles, or about 40 per cent of the original mileage.

In the immediate post-war period the Hull line and the Niagara Falls line of the Niagara, St. Catharines and Toronto (previously discontinued and then restored to service) were discontinued (1947), and in 1949 British Columbia Electric eliminated passenger service on its long line up the Fraser Valley. Additional portions of the

St. Catharines road went out in 1950. All lines were faced with continually falling passenger traffic as motor vehicle use became increasingly widespread, and rising costs of operating compared to passenger fares made the passenger service increasingly unprofitable. Freight traffic held up much better, but some roads experienced losses of traffic in this field as well. Thus in the seven-year period from 1952 to 1959, one by one the roads eliminated passenger service, and in a few instances all operations. British Columbia Electric cut back slowly in a planned programme of conversion to buses; most of the passenger service was out by 1955, although one line lasted until 1958. In 1955 came the end of passenger service on the two CPR lines in the Grand Valley; in 1956 the entire abandonment of the Montreal and Southern Counties as a separate road; in 1957 the discontinuance of passenger service on the London and Port Stanley; and in March 1959 the end of the last two passenger operations—the Quebec and the Thorold–Port Colborne services. The Port Colborne operation was a real curiosity in its last years of operation: although it was basically no different from hundreds of other lines in the United States and Canada that had been abandoned decades before, it ran on year after year, to the point at which it became something of a tourist attraction for persons from both countries interested in transportation history.

## THE CAUSES OF THE DECLINE

The disappearance of the intercity electric railway industry can be explained, of course, primarily in terms of the motor vehicle. Table IX shows the growth in motor vehicle use in Canada in the period 1903–60. For most of the travel for which the electric railway was suitable, the automobile offered still greater advantages in the form of flexibility and convenience, so that once car usage became general a large portion of the railway traffic disappeared. In some instances the loss was aggravated by bus competition. As noted in chapter IV, the policies of the provinces differed on the question of bus competition, but a number of lines suffered for a time—the Hamilton, Grimsby and Beamsville, the Hamilton and Dundas, the Chatham, Wallaceburg and Lake Erie, parts of Toronto Suburban, and others. Uitimately, with the decline in traffic and relatively lower costs of bus operation, bus service became more economical than continued operation of the rail passenger service.

In only one type of operation did electric rail passenger service offer an advantage, namely, in private-right-of-way service into large metropolitan areas. But in Toronto the electric lines had no such access to the downtown area, and other cities that had electric lines were not large enough to present sufficient traffic problems to give the rail lines an advantage. The one instance in which preservation of private right-of-way lines might have been advantageous from a long-range standpoint was Vancouver.

In the freight traffic field, the electric railway was particularly vulnerable to trucking for the type of traffic in which it first specialized, that is, merchandise freight, milk, fruit, and the like, where speed is of great importance. The greater flexibility of the truck allowed still greater speed and lessened rehandling. Thus, the electric lines lost most of this traffic even in the early days of the trucking industry. But carload freight traffic, much of it handled in conjunction with the steam railroads in long-distance movements, was much less vulnerable to trucking, although some shifting has occurred over the years. In the handling of this traffic the electric roads did not differ from the main line roads except in the somewhat incidental feature of the use of electric power.

## TABLE IX

Total Motor Vehicle Registrations in Canada in Selected Years,
1903–1953

| Year | Thousands of motor vehicles registered |
|------|----------------------------------------|
| 1903 | — |
| 1906 | 1 |
| 1909 | 5 |
| 1912 | 36 |
| 1915 | 95 |
| 1918 | 277 |
| 1921 | 465 |
| 1924 | 645 |
| 1927 | 940 |
| 1930 | 1,233 |
| 1931 | 1,201 |
| 1932 | 1,114 |
| 1933 | 1,083 |
| 1934 | 1,130 |
| 1935 | 1,176 |
| 1936 | 1,240 |
| 1937 | 1,320 |
| 1938 | 1,395 |
| 1939 | 1,439 |
| 1940 | 1,501 |
| 1941 | 1,573 |
| 1942 | 1,524 |
| 1943 | 1,512 |
| 1944 | 1,503 |
| 1945 | 1,497 |
| 1946 | 1,623 |
| 1947 | 1,836 |
| 1948 | 2,035 |
| 1949 | 2,291 |
| 1950 | 2,601 |
| 1951 | 2,872 |
| 1952 | 3,156 |
| 1953 | 3,431 |
| 1954 | 3,645 |
| 1955 | 3,949 |
| 1956 | 4,265 |
| 1957 | 4,497 |
| 1958 | 4,724 |
| 1959 | 5,018 |
| 1960 | 5,256 |

Source: Dominion Bureau of Statistics, *The Motor Vehicle* (Ottawa, annually).

One other factor played a part in the decline of the industry, namely, the inability to increase productivity per worker to a degree comparable to that in other industries. This is a common characteristic of the service industries, and has been a major source of difficulty for railroad main line and commuter passenger service. If productivity per man does not increase as much as is typical in industry, the prices of the service must rise more rapidly than the general price level if the industry is to continue to cover costs. But this was, of course, not feasible with the electric railways, in light of the high elasticity of demand produced by the availability of other forms of transport. Some of the last lines to be operated, and particularly the suburban lines of British

Columbia Electric, had far greater traffic density than the typical intercity line operated profitably in 1905 or 1910. But wage-fare relationships were such that operation was no longer profitable.

Although abandonment of the lines or of passenger service was basically a result of unsatisfactory earnings situations, the final decision was often precipitated by some event that necessitated substantial expenditures to keep the line operating. The need for changing the arc rectifiers from 25 to 60 cycles at a cost of some $60,000 brought the London and Port Stanley passenger service to an end. Montreal and Southern Counties was abandoned to avoid substantial expenditures necessitated by changes in the Victoria Bridge due to the St. Lawrence seaway development. Niagara Falls Park and River came to an end as its contract for operation with the Niagara Parks Commission terminated. The lines from Hamilton to Brantford and Beamsville were abandoned to permit their owners to sell their bus service free of electric railway competition.

Final operations of the Chatham, Wallaceburg and Lake Erie and the original Merritton line of the Niagara, St. Catharines and Toronto were ended by the insistence of municipal governments involved. In a few cases abandonment was decided upon on the basis of a careful calculation of earnings as compared to potential interest return on the salvage value of the property. Salvage value typically represented a small portion of the original cost, despite increased prices. A good figure was $8,000 a mile, much of this coming from the copper wire. In other cases it was obvious that the line operated essentially until it could no longer meet its expenses—the London and Lake Erie, for example.

## CHAPTER EIGHT

## CANADIAN AND UNITED STATES
## EXPERIENCE CONTRASTED

THE INTERCITY ELECTRIC railway developed more or less simultaneously in Canada and the United States. Although the basic inventions of the electric street car were made in the United States (and Germany), some of the earliest applications were at the Toronto Exhibition in 1884 and 1885 and in Windsor. The St. Catharines–Thorold line was in a sense the first intercity electric road in either country, and was built two years before the line generally considered the first United States interurban, that from Newark to Granville, Ohio (1889), But after 1900 Canadian development definitely lagged behind that in the United States; the greatest boom in United States construction from 1901 through 1903 had no Canadian counterpart at all. A much higher percentage (44 in contrast to 25) of the total Canadian mileage was built after 1910. On the other hand, although there was little construction in either country after 1917, there was a little more, relatively, in the United States than in Canada.

The abandonment pattern was likewise similar up through the mid-thirties, the peak period being 1931–32 in both countries. However, the mileage in Canada stabilized in the pre-1954 period to a much greater extent than in the United States where abandonments proceeded at a very rapid pace. As a consequence by the early fifties there were as many, and for a short time more, passenger carrying intercity electric railways in Canada than in the United States (although the mileage was somewhat less). Of the Canadian lines that survived after 1935, their vitality, particularly as passenger carriers, was surprisingly greater than in the United States. A partial explanation was government ownership of many of the Canadian ones, and thus both the greater pressure to continue operation as well as means of financing deficits. However, after 1954 the Canadian lines' passenger service vanished very rapidly.

When financial statistics are compared, the general results in Canada were not basically different from those in the United States. Operating ratios climbed steadily in both countries from the earliest years, but were consistently higher in Canada by about five points. The reason was apparently a greater traffic density per mile in the United States. However, in the period between 1902 and 1917 the Canadian lines showed a somewhat better rate of return on investment than their United States counterparts, despite the higher operating ratio. A portion, or perhaps even all, of this difference may be accounted for by the fact that there was less adjustment of United States investment figures to eliminate water. In any event, the figures are not substantially different. United States data are included in Table VI for purposes of comparison.

From a physical standpoint the Canadian and United States lines were much alike, and firms in both countries were well aware of technical developments in the other. Although most of the cars used in Canada were Canadian built and had some unique features in design, they were largely patterned after United States equipment. Virtually all the electrical equipment for the Canadian cars and substations was made in

Canada (by Westinghouse, and by Canadian General Electric in its Peterborough plants) but by subsidiaries of American companies and to American specifications. The Canadian lines were themselves Canadian owned, with minor exceptions; indeed, this was one Canadian industry that in itself was never dominated by the United States, although there was considerable influence from that country in early years.

# PART II

## THE INDIVIDUAL COMPANIES

## CHAPTER NINE

## ONTARIO

WITH EIGHTEEN COMPANIES and 553 miles of line, Ontario had a large portion of the total operations, even more than would have been expected in light of economic conditions. But even in Ontario there was no integrated network, and although in several instances, particularly in Hamilton, separate lines did connect it was impossible to travel any lengthy distance.

### THE DOMINION POWER COMPANY HAMILTON RADIALS[1]

Hamilton, rather than either of the two major metropolitan centres in Canada, had the greatest number of radial lines extending outward from it. There were four lines, all subsidiaries, except in their early years, of the Dominion Power and Transmission Company, which also owned the Hamilton street railway system and provided electric power in the area. Dominion Power was formed in 1907 as the successor to Hamilton Cataract Power Light and Traction Company; the latter, in turn, had been formed in 1903 to bring the various power and traction properties in the Hamilton area under common control. The enterprise had been developed by five Hamilton business men, all with the first name of John—Moodie, Gibson, Patterson, Sutherland, and Dickenson. Not until the early twenties did the control pass into other hands (the Power Company of Canada, the Nesbitt–Thomson interests). In April of 1930 the properties were acquired by the Ontario Hydro-Electric Power Commission, which operated the remaining radial lines for only a short time before abandoning them.

In the period around 1907 Dominion Power became seriously interested in developing and expanding the radial lines, and projected a through route from Toronto via Hamilton and London to Windsor. It completed the Brantford line and extended the Radial to Oakville, but at this point expansion ceased, and the great ambitions were never realized. The four radials were technically separate companies, with distinct names and equipment, but common management, integrated operation, and interchange of cars. All cars reached downtown Hamilton via streets; frequently cars coming in on one line would go directly out on another. A large $250,000 station completed in 1907 on King Street East, near the centre of the business area, served all lines; the structure stood until 1959. Power was provided from a hydro-electric generating plant at DeCew Falls near St. Catharines; conversion to DC took place at three substations in Hamilton. There were additional substations in Burlington and Oakville on the Radial, in Beamsville, Grimsby, and Stony Creek on the Beamsville line, and in Ancaster, Langford Siding, and Brantford on the Brantford line.

### Hamilton, Grimsby and Beamsville Electric Railway Company[2]

The oldest of the Hamilton electric lines, and one of the oldest in Canada, was the Hamilton, Grimsby and Beamsville, incorporated in 1895, and completed to Grimsby,

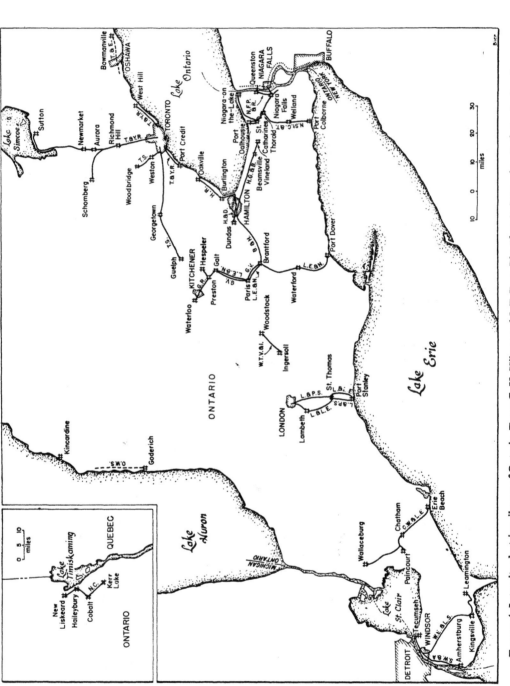

FIGURE 4. Intercity electric railways of Ontario. From G. H. Hilton and J. F. Due, *The Electric Interurban Railways in America* (Stanford, 1960.)

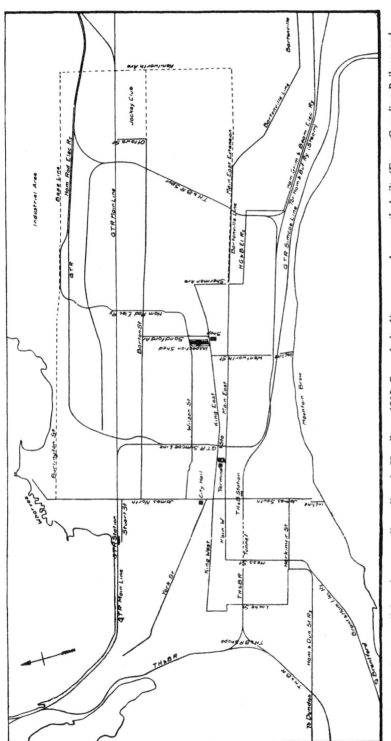

FIGURE 5. Street, radial, and steam railway lines in Hamilton, 1913. Several city lines were subsequently built. (From *Canadian Railway and Marine World*, June 1913, p. 282.)

twenty-two miles, in 1896 at a reported cost of only $271,707! Seventeen miles were in operation by June, the five remainder later in the year. The line was built along the edge of the highway right of way throughout, except for a short distance outside of Grimsby, where it turned towards the lake and thence into the centre of town. A steam generating station was built at Stoney Creek, but was later replaced by hydro power. The car house was at Grimsby. Eight cars, some 28 feet, some 36 feet, were acquired, powered with two 39-horsepower no. 12 Westinghouse motors.

Because of the numerous sharp curves and driveway crossings, speed was always limited (typically averaging fifteen miles an hour), and the standards of performance were not comparable to those of later lines. The rail was only fifty pound, and there were grades up to 4 per cent. But the area served was thickly settled, and the road developed a substantial passenger business. In addition, fruit orchards provided freight traffic, largely in small shipments to Hamilton, and milk business developed. Ultimately, carload traffic from canneries, several of which had no other rail connections, became important. As early as 1897 the road reported 170,000 separate shipments of fruit. Freight revenues averaged from 10 to 20 per cent of gross, unusual for an electric line in the pre–1910 period. Down until 1904 the road enjoyed an operating ratio of around 50 per cent, and a rate of return rarely less than 8 per cent up until 1915; in 1901 it reached 18 per cent.

The ultimate goal of the road was St. Catharines, and in 1904 an extension was completed beyond Beamsville to Vineland. The Niagara, St. Catharines and Toronto had planned to build a connection to Vineland, but abandoned the plans in 1905 when ownership changed. Its new owners developed plans for a high-speed line to Toronto, and thus lost interest in the HG&B, which would be paralleled. The HG&B operated its Vineland line for only one year; in May 1905 it announced abandonment of the line in light of losses of $7 a day and certain law suits from adjacent property owners, and, as soon as the fruit season was over in the fall, over protests of local residents operations were cut back to the east boundary of Beamsville and the remainder of the line dismantled. This was the first abandonment in Canada or the United States of a regularly operated intercity electric line.

In 1904 reports circulated that the line had been acquired by the Grand Trunk, but the following year Hamilton Cataract Power was revealed as the purchaser, and operations were co-ordinated with those of the other power company lines. Minority stockholders complained bitterly of the purchase terms, but to no avail.

For the next twenty years the operations continued largely unchanged, the only excitement being a protracted court case over the authority of the Ontario Railway Board to order the installation of lavatories on the cars. From 1905 on the operating ratio gradually rose as expenses outpaced revenues, but the rate of return continued reasonably adequate (5 to 7 per cent) until 1916. Traffic increased immediately after World War I, and passenger volume reached its peak in 1921. But costs had increased faster than revenues, and operating deficits appeared in 1921. Passenger volume fell slowly during the twenties, and freight traffic, much of it very vulnerable to truck competition, dropped in half. Bus competition, which commenced in 1922, aggravated the decline in traffic, but in 1927 Dominion Power purchased the bus line and co-ordinated service, and in that year the road earned its first profit since 1921. Fares were raised in 1929. When the depression came, the traffic fell drastically.

In 1930 the property passed with its parent power company into the hands of Ontario Hydro. Plans to abandon the property were announced in January 1931, but upon complaints of the municipalities operations were extended until June 30 of that year. Final action to abandon was precipitated by Hydro's sale of the bus routes to private interests on terms that required elimination of electric railway competition. Efforts of Hamilton to recover the $25,000 subsidy given in 1896 plus interest were unavailing. The line was dismantled in 1932, although certain spur lines were taken over by Canadian National to insure continued service to canneries.

The road operated for a total of thirty-nine years; it earned a return of 5 per cent or better in sixteen years, and operated at a deficit for ten years. Built to the essentially street car standards of the pre-1900 period, it enjoyed sufficient traffic to earn a good return on its low investment until the motor vehicle developed. But it was particularly vulnerable to motor competition because of the slow speed of its cars, the short distances travelled by most passengers, and the short haul, small-lot nature of its freight business. Had it not been for the willingness of the relatively profitable parent company to meet the deficits, it would likely have been abandoned in the early twenties.

### Hamilton and Dundas Street Railway Company

The second oldest and the shortest of the Dominion Power electric lines connected Hamilton with the old town of Dundas, with seven miles of line largely on private right of way. The line was built in 1876 as a steam road, and electrification was undertaken in 1897. Freight service was operated over the Dundas end of the line by the Toronto, Hamilton and Buffalo under a trackage rights agreement to provide downtown Dundas with its only rail outlet. The line extended from the King street terminal in Hamilton via Main, James South, and Herkimer streets, and thence along the highway to Dundas. In 1913, eighteen runs a day were provided. Considerable local traffic was handled in Hamilton.

Passenger traffic grew steadily on the line from 165,000 in 1898 to 1,150,000 in 1920, the peak year. The earnings were very stable, but not spectacular; the return on investment ranged from 4 to 6 per cent prior to 1909, and was almost as good down through 1919. Dividends were paid in several years in this period. But traffic dropped sharply as a result of bus and automobile competition after 1920, and the 1923 volume was only half that of 1920. The bus lines had a better, more direct route. Deficits appeared in 1920 and continued until abandonment. The operating deficit reached $25,000 in 1922, and in January 1923 the company announced plans to abandon service at the end of the month. As a result of protests operations were extended several times, finally coming to an end September 5, 1923. Private bus lines took over the service. Much of the intercity track was acquired by the Toronto, Hamilton and Buffalo for continuation of freight service, and most of the track in Hamilton by the Hamilton Street Railway.

The company operated as an electric line for twenty-six years, earning a return of 5 per cent or better in ten of these, and suffering an operating deficit only in the last three.

### Hamilton Radial Electric Company[3]

Hamilton Radial was incorporated in 1893, and at an early date passed into the hands of Hamilton Cataract Power. Eleven miles of line from downtown Hamilton via Burlington Beach to the town of Burlington were completed in 1897, and the track extended to Port Nelson the following year. From the business district the line followed King Street East to Sanford Avenue. and thence ran on its own right of way to the beach, close to the bay shore. It operated through the beach area on highway right of way and crossed the highway bridge over the canal that leads into Hamilton Harbour. In 1905 and 1906, at the height of radial expansion by the parent power company, the line was extended thirteen miles to Oakville, running on a private right of way parallel to the highway for most of the distance with grading for a second track that was never laid. The new line was opened for service May 3, 1906. Frequent service was operated to Burlington, particularly to the beach resort in the summer months. Numerous extra cars at short intervals were required for the week-end rushes of traffic, but the cars were not equipped for multiple-unit operation. The line beyond Burlington carried much less traffic, and service was less frequent. The road owned seven double end cars in 1913. Freight traffic was negligible, except for a small amount of carload switching to industrial sidings on the line in Hamilton.

Hamilton Radial showed a reasonably adequate return on investment (around 6 per cent) until the Oakville extension was built; this more than doubled investment but did not affect absolute net profit, and thus the return fell more than half, reaching 2 per cent in 1909. It recovered to 5 per cent in the years 1911–13 and then fell sharply again. The figure was less than typical for the industry as a whole throughout the period after 1906. The peak year for passenger volume was 1913, the earliest of any road, and the decline was more or less continuous; in 1921, the year in which many roads reached their peak, the figure was half that of 1913. The 1928 figure was less than one-third that of 1913.

In 1918, the road obtained approval from the Board of Railway Commissioners for a rate increase. But by specific requirement of the company's incorporating act, sanction by the municipalities was also necessary. When Burlington flatly refused the company curtailed service, and when the town attempted to force restoration of the old schedule the company ceased all operations on December 13, 1918. The municipalities appealed to the Board of Railway Commissioners, which notified them that it could take no further action in light of the losses. The company made plans to liquidate, but finally, following a municipal election and change in administration, Burlington gave in on the fare increase, and service was restored February 5, 1919. [4]

The continued decline in traffic from automobile use brought an operating deficit in 1918 and in very year except one between 1920 and 1927. The light-traffic northern section between Burlington and Oakville was abandoned on August 3, 1925, and as a consequence, a slight operating profit was earned the following year. Business continued to decline, however, and the remainder of the line was abandoned January 5, 1929. [5] Buses replaced the cars on the Hamilton–Burlington service. Three miles of track in Hamilton were kept in carload freight service until July 13, 1931, when operation of the segment was taken over by the Canadian National and the Toronto, Hamilton and Buffalo. A portion of the trackage in the city was operated by Hamilton Street Railway until 1951.

The Radial operated for twenty-six years, suffering deficits in eight of these, with a rate of return in excess of 5 per cent in ten years, almost solely in the early period. The road was moderately successful as a suburban carrier; it was ruined, financially, by the Oakville extension. On a number of occasions plans were developed to bridge the eleven-mile gap between Oakville and the Toronto and York Radial's line at Port Credit, to provide a through route from Hamilton to Toronto. Surveys were made, but no construction was ever started because without substantial rebuilding the route would have been too slow to have permitted much through traffic. The Hydro radial plans of the 1920 period also called for such a line, either utilizing the

Hamilton Radial route north of Burlington or paralleling it, but these plans of course did not materialize.

*Brantford and Hamilton Electric Railway Company*[6]

The last of the Hamilton lines, and the only one built to relatively high standards throughout, was the Brantford and Hamilton, which connected the two cities in its name. The road was incorporated in 1904 by the Von Echa interests of Pennsylvania (which controlled the Brantford city lines and the Grand Valley) to build from Toronto to Detroit. The charter was awarded only after the Hamilton, Ancaster and Brantford, chartered several years before by the Haines group of New York City, had failed to get the first five miles of track built in the prescribed time. Construction of the B&H from Hamilton was commenced late in 1906; early in 1908 service was opened to Ancaster, and on June 1, 1908, the entire twenty-three mile line from Hamilton to Brantford was placed in service. Meanwhile, control had first passed to an Indianapolis group headed by W. L. Taylor, and then, prior to completion, to Hamilton Cataract Power. In 1916 the track was extended one mile in Brantford to reach the new Union Station built in conjunction with the Lake Erie and Northern.

The B&H was a well built private-right-of-way line, with extensive grading and cuts and 80-pound rail. The cars left Hamilton on Main and Hess streets, went onto a private right of way just beyond Herkimer street, and climbed the mountain on a long continuous grade of $2\frac{1}{2}$ per cent. The track paralleled what is now highway 2 as far as Ancaster, and then ran north of the highway to a point near Alberton. Here it crossed the highway and the Toronto, Hamilton and Buffalo tracks on an overhead crossing and ran almost straight to Cainsville, then on into Brantford, entering the city along the old canal on the south edge of town. For many years hourly service was provided, with six heavy 56-foot Kuhlman cars purchased when the road was built. After 1929 cars were alternated with buses operated by the company. Freight traffic was light, limited mainly to package freight, and largely disappeared after 1921.

Passenger traffic grew steadily, from 373,000 in 1909 to a peak of 861,000 in 1920; the traffic was less suburban in character than that of the other three Hamilton roads, and many passengers travelled between the terminal cities. Built relatively late, and at a higher cost per mile than its cousins, the B&H showed a rate of return of only from 2 to 4 per cent in its early years. Then came four very good years, 1918–21 inclusive, with returns of 7 to 8 per cent. The decline began in 1921, and traffic fell steadily to a 1928 figure less than half the 1920 peak. During these years operating expenses were barely covered. Then came—for reasons not obvious—one last good year, 1929. But the depression cut revenues drastically, and two years of small operating deficits followed.

In April 1930 the line passed into the hands of Ontario Hydro, which operated it until abandonment on June 30, 1931, the same date the Hamilton–Beamsville line was discontinued. Abandonment was precipitated by Hydro's sale of bus rights on terms that stipulated exclusion of electric railway competition. The earnings position of the road was actually better than that of many other lines, and the line might have continued in operation for several more years, perhaps until after 1945, under other circumstances of ownership. The contrast between the B&H and the HG&B is interesting; with its heavy investment the Brantford line was unable to show as good earnings as the Beamsville road in the earlier years, but its higher speed and longer distance travel enabled it to continue to gain business and cover its expenses after the other road was suffering operating deficits. In total, it operated twenty-three years, with earnings over 5 per cent in five years, and deficits in only two, the last years of operation.

## THE WINDSOR AND CHATHAM AREA ROADS

The most southerly section of western Ontario contained three interurbans, two operating out of Windsor, the third north and south from Chatham.

### Sandwich, Windsor and Ahmerstburg Railway Company

As noted in part I, the first electric street car line in Canada operated in Windsor. On June 6, 1886, at a time when there were no more than seven electric car lines, all very short, in operation in the United States,[7] service began on a two-mile line extending from downtown Windsor to the Walkerville area. The line had two electric passenger cars, each with one motor mounted on the platform of the car, and connected by a chain belt to the axle, running on rails consisting of iron strips laid on stringers. Cars left each end of the line every half hour. The enterprise was promoted by J. W. Tringham until his death in 1887 when control passed to W. M. Boomer. There are conflicting reports about the success of operation. Boomer, in a letter to the *Street Railway Journal* in May 1887, reported that the line had run successfully for the last year, and Van Depoele, who had installed the system, listed it on several occasions as one of his successful undertakings. It was reported that the line had paid for itself in two years, and was carrying 200,000 passengers per year. The company, reorganized as the Windsor Electric Street Railway Company, did not expand its electrification, however, and until 1891 most service in the city was still provided by the old horse-car company, a separate enterprise. It is not entirely clear that the electric operation was even continuous over this period. In 1891, a new enterprise with the name of the Windsor, Sandwich and Amherstburg Railway Company was formed under different control, and proceeded to electrify and extend the horse-car lines and to absorb the Walkerville line. This road was eventually reorganized as the Sandwich, Windsor and Amherstburg.

Out of this city system grew two interurban routes. In 1901 the company came under control of its big neighbour across the river, Detroit United, which had been formed early in the year as a merger of the Wilson-Johnson and Everett-Moore systems in that city under control of the latter. This syndicate operated much of the interurban network of northern Ohio, as well as the London Street Railway. There was some affiliation between the Everett–Moore and Mackenzie–Mann interests, and considerable Montreal capital had been invested in Detroit United. In 1915 control passed into Montreal hands.

Following the transfer of control to Detroit United in 1901, construction was started on the fourteen-mile line to Amherstburg, which was completed and placed in service June 10, 1903. In 1907, a new company, the Windsor and Tecumseh, commenced to build to Tecumseh town; the six-mile road was taken over by SW&A and completed in the same year. The W&T retained its corporate identity for many years, but was operated as a portion of the SW&A. The Amherstburg line came from downtown Windsor on city streets, swung close to the river near Sunnyside, turned inland again to miss a marshy area, returned to the river bank several miles north of Amherstburg, and followed the river to a point near the edge of town where it turned inland to reach the downtown area. The Tecumseh line paralleled the river through Walkerville to a point directly north of Tecumseh, and then turned sharply to follow a county road southward into the town. This was little more than a suburban operation.

The life of the SW&A as a private company was not a happy one. The municipalities, particularly Windsor, and the company engaged in an endless wrangle over street paving, extensions, and other matters, and, just as in Detroit, municipal purchase was discussed for a decade. As one consequence of these difficulties the company allowed the system to deteriorate. When the franchise expired, the municipalities, after overwhelming approval by the voters in an election on December 6, 1919, purchased the system for $2,039,000, and took control March 31, 1920. Under the terms of the Ontario radial legislation, the municipalities contracted with Ontario Hydro for operation. Bonds for the purchase were issued by Hydro and secured by debentures issued by the municipalities with provincial guarantee. During the period of Hydro operation, the line was known as the Essex Division, Hydro-Electric Railways.

The badly deteriorated property was rebuilt, and new equipment obtained. Among the cars purchased were twelve which came in 1924 and 1925 from the Ottawa Car Company and which were identical with eight cars for the suburban lines of the former Toronto and York Radial. These were among the few modern lightweight cars (prior to the PCC car) ever used in Canada for urban service; with a capacity of forty-four, they weighed only 44,000 pounds and were 45 feet long. They were equipped for multiple operation with Tomlinson couplers, but normally were used as single units; by the nature of the traffic, multiple-unit service was not advantageous. These cars provided service until the end of operations.

The road soon became a model of Hydro radial operation, and passenger traffic rose with the rapid growth of population in the area. Local freight business, negligible until 1922, increased on the interurban lines. In 1922 it was reported that four new sidings were laid down to the edge of the Detroit River to facilitate "export" of beer from Walkerville to the United States, and a year later, it was reported that the road was handling 10,000 cases of beer a day—or more correctly—per night. The beer was unloaded from the line's freight cars into boats at the river edge for delivery on the other side of the river—provided the boats were not intercepted first by the United States Coast Guard. Little carload interchange business was ever conducted. After 1928 freight traffic fell drastically.

The depression of the thirties struck the Windsor area very severely, and after 1931 the profits quickly turned to small operating losses, leaving the municipalities saddled with the interest charges. In 1931, in terms of changed provincial legislation, the province withdrew from financial participation. The municipalities then formed the Sandwich, Windsor and Amherstburg Railway Company, which took over ownership and again contracted for Hydro operation. Several of the municipalities defaulted on their obligations, and the burden passed onto the remaining ones involved. Vigorous appeals were made for provincial assistance to meet the obligations. In 1934, Ontario Hydro suddenly cancelled its contract for operations on the grounds that the municipalities were not meeting their obligations to it, and washed its hands of the whole deal.[8] The municipalities then took over direct management and operation of the line. In 1937 the new chairman of the local commission investigated the road's operations as well as Detroit's experience, and decided that rail service should be abandoned. The Amherstburg line was replaced by buses on March 21, 1938, and the Tecumseh line on May 15. The SW&A was still operating bus service in the Windsor area in 1965.

In 1949 the Ontario government enacted legislation to clear up the debt situation. Five towns and two townships were freed of their obligations for $1,098,137 of bonds outstanding, and Windsor's obligations were essentially reduced from over $4 million to $1.5 million. The railway (now bus) company assumed principal and interest of $2.1 million, interest on an additional $9 million, and agreed to compensate the province for some $1.5 million in bonds which the latter had paid. The net effect was that the province did bear a portion of the debt, and the transit system was ultimately able to pay off much of the remainder.

### Windsor, Essex and Lake Shore Rapid Railway Company[9]

The Windsor, Essex and Lake Shore, built at a later date than the Amherstburg line, was characterized by higher standards of operation, and was a truly intercity line rather than a primarily suburban operation. Except for its last two years under Hydro management it was completely independent of the SW&A in both financial and operating aspects.

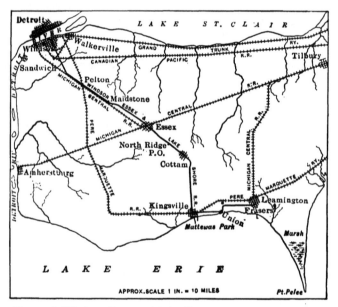

FIGURE 6. Windsor, Essex and Lake Shore Railway. (*From Electric Railway Journal*, Nov. 30, 1912, p. 1096.)

The line was promoted shortly after 1900 by W. Newman, city engineer of Windsor, together with A. J. Nelles. A charter was obtained in 1901, and after long difficulty in arranging finances American capital was obtained, and construction was started in 1905 by the Keystone Construction Company of Philadelphia. When this company ran into financial difficulties, control of the undertaking was transferred to the Ontario construction firm of J. Piggott and Sons, which then completed the line. Construction was held up for several months at Essex when the Michigan Central refused to permit the line to cross, but finally a crossing was ordered by the Board of Railway Commissioners after the WE&LS had demonstrated that a subway was impracticable because of drainage problems. In 1907 service was opened to Kingsville (twenty-seven miles) and on April 10, 1908, to Leamington (thirty-six miles from Windsor).

The line commenced in downtown Windsor, reached the outskirts by street running, and thence operated on its own right of way, paralleling the Michigan Central (on the east side) to Essex, where it crossed the steam line, followed the Leamington highway to a point just beyond Cottam, and turned straight south into Kingsville. Beyond Kingsville the line followed the shore highway to a point south of Ruthven, turned north into the town, swung southeast again towards the lake shore, and once again turned straight north to enter Leamington from the south on Erie Street. The track was well graded, laid (north of Kingsville) with eighty-pound rail. Most was level but there was a 5 per cent grade in Kingsville.

The WE&LS was Canada's only single-phase AC line—a power system subjected to extensive experimentation in the United States shortly after 1900 in an effort to avoid the voltage drop and need for frequent substations of the traditional 600-volt DC. Twenty-five cycle AC current was fed into the line (of catenary construction) at 6,600 volts at Kingsville, with one substation in Maidstone. Heavy steel frame cars were obtained from the Ottawa Car Company with pantograph contact, the first on intercity lines in Canada. Each car had two 160-horsepower Westinghouse motors. The cars were named, an unusual practice. Typically nine trains a day each way were operated. For a time two ran as limiteds in 85 minutes, in contrast to the 105 minutes of the locals.

Passenger traffic grew steadily, from about 300,000 in 1910 to over 900,000 in the peak year, 1921. Substantial beach traffic to Mattewas Park on the lake at Kingsville developed, and in the winter there was special theatre service to Detroit. The two major towns, Kingsville and Leamington, had little steam rail passenger service, and thus a substantial portion of the traffic went through from Windsor to these towns. Some carload and package freight was handled, but rarely provided more than 25 per cent of total revenue. The rate of return of the road was remarkably good up through 1921, exceeding 5 per cent in every year except 1910 and 1918, and ranging from 7 to 9 per cent in most of the years.

As the automobile developed, passenger traffic fell sharply after 1923, and by 1928 was less than a third of the peak year (1921). To ward off competition, co-ordinated bus service was introduced in 1925 and extended for a time to Chatham, but it was not profitable, so was discontinued in 1927 upon assurance from the province that no competing service would be permitted. Operations in the late twenties were carried on exactly as they had been two decades before. The ponderous old cars were capable of high speed once they got under way, but their AC motors seriously restricted their acceleration rate and hampered the development of suburban business out of Windsor, and their excessive weight caused unnecessary damage to the tracks. Although most United States lines had long ago dropped single-phase AC operation because of its basic inefficiency and high maintenance costs, the WE&LS still employed it. Also other Ontario lines had shifted years before to the cheap hydro power, but the WE&LS still generated its own in its Kingsville plant, the two dynamos driven by antiquated cross-compound steam engines. Its power costs were 15 cents a train mile, compared to 7 cents for the SW&A. The company was still controlled by the same interests, its stock and bonds technically owned by Dominion Traction and Light whose only other property was the Windsor Gas Company.

Operating losses commenced in 1927, and in that year the owners notified the municipalities that they were unable to continue to operate the road, and offered

F

to sell the property for estimated salvage value, $296,000, for municipal operation. The municipalities (all except three small ones) voted approval in 1928,[10] and after prolonged negotiations and after the municipalities had approved the debentures and enacted the necessary bylaws the property was finally transferred on September 8, 1929.

As planned when the purchase was contemplated, the system was immediately modernized under Hydro supervision. Track was rebuilt, new poles installed, operations converted to 600-volt DC with Hydro power, substations built, and five new cars purchased. Four were motor cars, built to modern lightweight standards and seating fifty passengers, and the fifth was a parlour car. All were labelled "The Sunshine County Route." Operation was carried on under contract by Hydro and co-ordinated to some extent with the SW&A operation. About $700,000 of the total cost of $1,100,000 for modernization was provided through debentures issued by the municipalities, Windsor's share being $316,000.

The purchase and modernization occurred, of course, at exactly the wrong time, because it was scarcely completed when the effects of the depression reduced revenue still more and increased operating losses. Within a year, there was talk of abandonment, and by 1932 accumulated deficits after fixed charges had reached $109,000. In May of that year, representatives from the municipalities voted to abandon operations, although Windsor did not vote and Kingsville strongly opposed the move. Application to abandon was made to the Board of Railway Commissioners and the fact stressed that deficits had been incurred in every month except two since modernization. The line suspended service September 15, 1932. There was some talk of reviving operations, but nothing came of it. The cars were held in storage until sale to the Montreal and Southern Counties in 1939, and in 1935 the track was torn up. The municipalities were of course left with their debenture obligations. There followed a long and bitter series of discussions with the province, the municipalities claiming that they were deliberately misled by Hydro engineers with respect to potential profits, and demanding that the province assume the debt. The province refused to do so, pointing out that the initiative for the plan came from the municipalities. In 1959 some municipalities were still paying off the debt.

Although modernization was obviously foolish, and the municipalities and Hydro both had failed to recognize the long-term trends, once expenditures had been incurred the governments were obviously too hasty in seeking abandonment. They did not realize that most of the immediate difficulty was simply a product of the depression. Had they kept the line going a little longer, it would likely have recovered with improved business conditions, lasted through World War II at least, and returned some of the investment.

*Chatham, Wallaceburg and Lake Erie Railway Company*[11]

Chatham located roughly half way between London and Windsor, was the centre of operations of the Chatham, Wallaceburg and Lake Erie, which extended in almost a straight line southeastward from Wallaceburg to Erie Beach. The road was incorporated in 1903 by a group of Chatham investors, and headed for a number of years by D. A. Gordon, M.P. for East Kent. The line from Chatham to Wallaceburg (eighteen miles) was placed in operation on November 20, 1905, and that to Erie Beach (fifteen miles) in mid-1908. Completion of a subway under the Michigan Central tracks united the two lines on August 20, 1908. In 1909 a six-mile branch was built from a point on the Wallaceburg line a few miles north of Chatham to the little village of Paincourt, but a suit by a farmer held up operation until August 1910.

The northern line was designed to provide frequent service to Wallaceburg, a town isolated from main transportation routes by its location midway between the London–Sarnia and London–Detroit rail and highway routes. The line went northwest out of Chatham for two miles along highway 40, turned southwest for half a mile, and thence northwest through Dover Centre, running adjacent to the highway again for the last few miles into Wallaceburg. The Paincourt branch went off to the west at the point at which the main line turned north the second time. The southern

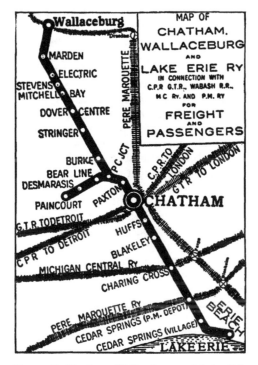

FIGURE 7. Chatham, Wallaceburg and Lake Erie Railway. (From *Canadian Railway and Marine World*, Oct. 1913, p. 493.)

line ran on a private right of way along the west edge of the highway from Chatham through Charing Cross and Cedar Springs to the lake shore, and thence turned eastward along the shore to Erie Beach. The two lines were connected by three miles of street running north and south through the business district of Chatham. The road was built primarily for passenger business of the usual pattern, plus summer excursion traffic to Lake Erie beaches. It also developed a considerable amount of freight traffic with the steam roads. There were freight interchanges with the Canadian Pacific and the Grand Trunk at Chatham, with the Michigan Central at Charing Cross, and the Pere Marquette at Cedar Springs, Chatham, and Wallaceburg. From 1911 on, one half or more of the gross revenue came from freight, and by the mid-twenties the ratio exceeded 75 per cent. In 1913 the control of the road was obtained by the Mackenzie–Mann interests, for reasons unknown.

The earnings of the road were more or less typical of the industry for most of the years, averaging about 5 per cent prior to 1918. But passenger traffic commenced to fall after 1914; the 1920 figure was less than half the peak, and the 1926 figure only 88,000, or 20 per cent of the peak. The result was a rapid decline in revenue, even though carload freight traffic continued to increase up to 1928. The earnings picture was very unsatisfactory from 1918 on, and operating deficits were incurred in five years in the period 1921–27.

It was apparent by 1920 that the road was in serious financial difficulties, and discussion arose about the possibility of sale to the municipalities for Hydro operation. The city of Chatham began to exert pressure to get the tracks off the Main Street through the building of a belt line, a move opposed by the merchants. By the mid-twenties bus competition had developed between Chatham and Wallaceburg, and attempts of the CW&LE to have it eliminated failed, partly because of the argument of Wallaceburg that the rail service was inadequate. In 1927 application was filed before the Board of Railway Commissioners to discontinue passenger service; when no immediate action was taken the company, announced discontinuance of passenger runs on July 2, 1927, order or no order, warning that if any attempt were made to stop this by legal action, all operations would cease.[12] Passenger service ended as announced, and in 1928 the board refused to order its restoration (34 CRC 116).

The road attempted to continue freight operations, but was harrassed by the city of Chatham. On August 17, 1927, all operations were ordered stopped by the Board of Railway Commissioners on the complaint from Chatham that the Thames bridge in the city was unsafe. Repairs were made, and freight service started again on September 2. In 1928 the company showed a modest operating profit; clearly the passenger service had not been covering its out-of-pocket cost. In 1929 Chatham ordered the line to build a belt route around the city, and when this project was not undertaken for lack of funds, the city cancelled the franchise on March 1, 1930, on the grounds that the track had not been maintained as required. The company did not contest the action, which was upheld by the Supreme Court of Ontario, and admitted default, and the city proceeded to tear up some of the trackage. Attempts to sell portions of the line to steam roads were unavailing, and the entire line was dismantled.


THE LONDON LINES

Although London was the planned destination of a number of lines, only two interurbans ever operated from it, one of which essentially drove the other out of business.

*South Western Traction Company (London and Lake Erie Railway and Transportation Company)*[13]

The initial request of the promoters of the South Western for a charter in 1900 was rejected by the Ontario legislature as a result of a vigorous protest from the city of London, owner of the steam-operated London and Port Stanley. However, the legislature reconsidered, the charter was granted, and construction was commenced in 1902 with funds that were provided by a syndicate of English business men. Track was laid as far as Lambeth in that year from the outskirts of London, but by this time the company was out of funds, and hampered by the inability to obtain a satisfactory entrance into London. Nothing was done in 1903; finally in 1904 additional English capital was obtained, and construction taken over by the Canadian Electric Traction Company of England. Arrangements were finally completed for an entrance into London, a bridge was built across the Thames, and the line extended southward. Early in 1906 the road was able to inaugurate service to Lambeth, and in June extended it to Talbotville and late in the year to St. Thomas. In November 1907 the line was completed to Port Stanley, twenty-eight miles from London. Originally the line was built for three-phase AC operation under the Ganz system developed in Budapest, but when this did not prove satisfactory it was replaced by 600-volt DC, apparently in the first year of operation.

The London terminal was on Horton Street in what became the Salvation Army hostel; the track ran parallel to Richmond Street and on the Base Line Road from the Thames River bridge through Lambeth, thence on adjacent private right of way to St. Thomas, and over the St. Thomas Street Railway trackage eastward on Talbot Street through the business district to the terminal next to the Clifton Hotel on Colborne Street. The company's own tracks started again on the eastern edge of town, turned straight south for a mile, and thence wound around in a crooked path through Union into Port Stanley. They kept to the east of the L&PS after the crossing in downtown St. Thomas.

The line, which throughout its life was called "The Traction Line", had scarcely been completed before it suffered a major blow—destruction of its barns and most of its cars by fire. By 1908 the company was in receivership, and it was sold at foreclosure on October 20, 1909, to J. E. MacDougall of London, and taken over by a Toronto group headed by G. B. Woods, who had also gained control of the Von Echa roads. The company was renamed the London and Lake Erie Railway and Transportation Company. Additional cars were obtained, and for a few years the company prospered, more than covering interest. A large volume of summer travel from London to the Lake Erie beaches developed, for which multiple-car trains were employed. In 1912 the road purchased two new 50-foot arched roof steel passenger cars with motors, and two trailers from Niles Car Company in Ohio; on occasion all four were used in a single train for beach traffic. In 1912 a long fight arose over the company's attempt to operate cars on Sunday, of particular importance because of the beach traffic. The line claimed that it was subject to exceptions in Dominion legislation relating to the applicability of laws restricting Sunday operation, and the Appellate Court of Ontario finally upheld its right to operate. Sunday operation, which had stopped June 30, 1912, resumed May 11, 1913. A small freight traffic yielded about 10 per cent of gross.

The line got off to a relatively poor start, but by 1909, earnings had reached 4 per cent on investment; through 1915 they averaged from 4 to 6 per cent, and the peak-year traffic (in 1914) was twice that of early years. But even this modest prosperity was short lived; the electrification of the L&PS quickly reduced the passenger traffic and gross revenue by half, because the L&LE, with its light track and cars, street operation, and roundabout route was no match for the modern, high-speed city-owned line. By 1917 it was obvious that operation could not be continued, and upon default of interest the bondholders took steps towards liquidation. Lengthy negotiations were carried on with the cities of London and St. Thomas over possible sale of the properties. London particularly was interested in keeping the northern portion of the line in operation as a suburban carrier, because the route was well removed from that of the L&PS. The company insisted on 60 cents on the dollar of investment, but the city of London would not go beyond 35 cents so no agreement was reached. Service was discontinued on October 15, 1918, and the line immediately scrapped.

## London and Port Stanley Railway Company[14]

The London and Port Stanley is one of the oldest railroads in Canada, but was electrified at a relatively late date. The plan for the line was sponsored in 1852 by a number of prominent London business men who sought a better outlet to the lake and feared Great Western monopoly rates. In 1853 the charter was obtained and construction started. The line was opened for service on September 25, 1856, with twenty-four miles of line, built to 5½-foot gauge, from London straight south through St. Thomas to the lake shore at Port Stanley. The volume of business was inadequate to make the road yield a profit, but it covered operating expenses and was important as a lever in holding down Great Western rates. Although the enterprise was privately promoted, individuals owned only a minority of the stock (£10,125), the rest being sold to the cities of London (£50,000) and St. Thomas (£8,500), and the counties of Elgin (£20,000) and Middlesex (£25,000). From 1855 to 1859 London loaned the road £105,000. In 1872 the property was leased for twenty years to the Great Western with a return of only about ½ per cent on the investment, and converted to standard gauge. Upon expiration of the lease, London, which owned most of the bonds but only a minority of the stock,[15] gained control by obtaining from the legislature voting power for the bonds on which interest had not been paid. The city then leased the road to the Lake Erie and Detroit River line (later Pere Marquette, now Cheasapeake and Ohio) for another twenty years. The primary functions of the road had become those of access to London for the Michigan Central (which operated over its line north of St. Thomas under trackage rights) and for the Pere Marquette, and of the prosaic job of hauling London's coal supply from the lake. By 1910 86 per cent of its freight tonnage was coal. Excursion traffic to the lakes was substantial.

The time of expiration of the second lease coincided with the development of interest in Ontario in a province-wide system of radial railways under Hydro sponsorship. Sir Adam Beck, whose home was in London, began in 1912 to urge electrification of the L&PS as an element in the system, and late in 1913 the project was approved by the voters. Thus the Pere Marquette lease was not renewed; the city leased the line beginning January 1, 1914 and had it rebuilt and electrified with 80-pound rail and a modern 1,500-volt DC system with catenary construction. Five steel motor cars, 59 feet in length, weighing 92,900 pounds, and equipped with four GE 125-horsepower motors and pantograph contact, were built for the line by the Jewett Car Company of Newark, Ohio. They were built to the railroad (monitor) roof design of the earlier cars, but with continuous structure members from one floor sill to another. Three wooden trailer cars were built by the Preston Car Company, and three by St. Louis. All cases were equipped for multiple operation, two-car trains being common, and up to six cars when travel to the beach was heavy. Hourly service was typical. Heavy electric locomotives were acquired for freight traffic. Passenger trains operated out of the Grand Trunk (later Canadian National) station in London, and the road's station in St. Thomas was in the centre of the business district. A secondary aspect of the road's passenger service was the provision of passenger connections from St. Thomas to the CPR and CNR at London, and, in reverse, to provide London connections with Michigan Central trains at St. Thomas.

Some L&PS connecting trains backed into Michigan Central's ancient station in St. Thomas. Virtually the entire line was on private right of way. In 1917, two 72-foot cars, nos. 12 and 14, were purchased, the largest interurban cars ever built for Canadian roads. These were intended as prototypes for the radial network then being planned in Ontario.

The road pushed its freight business vigorously, and negotiated through rates with the steam lines, ending the Michigan Central's operation over the line by virtue of trackage rights. Technically, the road was operated by the London Railway Commission under lease from the city-controlled railway company. In the early years of electrification the road prospered, and freight and passenger revenues were about equal. Passenger traffic in 1916 was about five times that of the old steam train service, and in 1921, by which time the London and Lake Erie line had been abandoned, the figure was twice that of 1916. Freight volume doubled from 1916 to 1929. Interest was covered annually until 1923, with an over-all rate of return ranging from 5 to 8 per cent, but in the next six years, although operating profits were earned, they constituted less than 5 per cent on investment, and thus interest was not covered. Because the line was municipally owned, virtually all the cost of electrification— about $1,900,000—had been covered by borrowing.

After 1921, the automobile commenced to reduce the passenger volume, which fell 40 per cent between 1921 to 1929. The industrial growth of London, however, kept freight revenues rising. The depression cut both freight and passenger revenues drastically, from $609,000 gross in 1929 to $281,000 in 1933. Small operating losses developed, and the city even considered abandonment. Freight decline was aggravated by the suspension of car ferry service to Port Stanley from Conneaut. However, with the recovery of the economy and the growth of gasoline traffic from new bulk plants erected at Port Stanley, the finances improved again, and from 1934 to 1958 an operating deficit was incurred in only one year, 1954. World War II brought an all-time passenger traffic record (the 1943 figure was 70 per cent greater than the previous peak in 1921). Freight traffic rose much less, the 1948 high being 30 per cent less than the 1929 peak, but the tonnage was relatively stable after 1943.

After 1950 the problem of continued operation of passenger service became a major controversy. Continued decline in business and rising costs relative to fares had rendered the service increasingly unprofitable, and the railroad management sought to discontinue it in 1952. Substantial opposition was aroused in London, and in 1953 voters rejected a proposal to sell the passenger rights to Greyhound for $100,000 and discontinue passenger service. Rail service was gradually reduced, however, and experiments with fare changes were not successful. By 1955, only 173,000 passengers were carried, 10 per cent of the 1943 peak, and the road as a whole was barely breaking even. A crisis was reached in 1956 when Ontario Hydro prepared to change the St. Thomas area power from 25 to 60 cycles. A substantial sum of money was required to change the line's rectifiers, and the city of London was unwilling to advance the sum. As a consequence, on February 1, 1957, passenger service came to an end south of St. Thomas and north of St. Thomas on February 18, with approval of the Board of Transport Commissioners over substantial opposition. Line freight operations were dieselized although up through 1963 electric power was still used for express service north of St. Thomas. In 1955 the old corporation was dissolved and direct ownership of the property was vested in the hands of the city of London. Early in 1965 the city indicated its intention to discontinue service.

The over-all record of the L&PS in its forty years of electric operation was not nearly as bad as newspaper accounts of the line have at times suggested. It earned from 5 to 8 per cent on investment in earlier years of electrification and, after three years of deficits, recovered to a return of from 2 to 3 per cent. It did well during World War II, and only after 1952 did it have difficulty in avoiding operating losses. In fifteen of the forty years of electrified operation it earned better than 5 per cent on its investment, and suffered operating deficits in only six years. For the thirty years, 1915–45, operating revenues totalled $13,325,659, operating expenses $10,864,515, surplus after rental and taxes $1,108,508, interest $2,550,936; the road earned about 3 per cent on investment over this period, covering about half its interest charge.

## LINES IN THE GRAND VALLEY

The valley of the Grand River has for many years been a centre of industrial activity in Ontario, in textiles, farm equipment, car building, industrial equipment, and other fields. The presence of a number of moderate-sized cities was a natural lure for interurban building, and allowed relatively successful operation of two roads.

### Grand River Railway Company[16]

The Grand River was one of Canada's first electric lines. The predecessor company, the Galt and Preston, was incorporated in 1890, and a line built between these two towns in 1893. Service was established on July 26, 1894. In 1896 the name was changed to the Galt, Preston and Hespeler as the extension to the latter town was completed in January, and operations were conducted under this name for several decades. The line was built on a private right of way, but had grades up to 5 per cent in earlier years. Operations began with four 37-foot motor cars and three trail cars. The other segment of the later GR was the Preston and Berlin, built from Preston to Berlin (now Kitchener) in 1903 (opened October 6). At a very early date these roads were purchased by the Canadian Pacific and their operations co-ordinated. In 1903 the CPR obtained a Dominion charter for a new enterprise called the Berlin, Waterloo, Wellesley, and Lake Huron, to which control of the two original companies was transferred in 1908, although both roads were operated under their old names. In 1914, the Grand River Railway Company was incorporated to take over the property of the BWW&LH, but it was not until 1918 that the name "Grand River Railway" was adopted for the properties and the original names discontinued. In 1906 a car barn fire destroyed most of the original equipment, and new cars were purchased. Modern equipment built by Preston Car and Coach Company was obtained in 1911 and 1921.

The GR developed a substantial volume of freight business, primarily carload interchange for the parent CPR, which did not reach the Kitchener area by its own rails. As early as 1895, it was handling CPR box cars to factory sidings on the lines with a light Baldwin steam locomotive and an electric freight motor. By 1907 freight was yielding over half the revenue, and by 1929 two-thirds. Passenger cars were operated on frequent intervals out of Galt on both lines, in the peak years hourly to Kitchener and Hespeler and every thirty minutes to Preston. Little change was made for many years, except for the building of a cutoff in Kitchener in 1921 to eliminate street running. The line was subjected to bus competition in the early twenties before effective regulation was established, and eventually introduced its own bus operations under the name of Canadian Pacific Transport. The peak rail passenger year was

1920, but the decline down to 1929 (about 30 per cent) was much less than on many lines. After World War II buses replaced most rail passenger service on the main line to Kitchener but frequent rail service still operated to Hespeler. Early applications to abandon all rail passenger service were rejected in 1950 and 1952, but a renewal of the application was granted in 1955, and all rail passenger service came to an end on April 24, 1955. Freight operation was continued with electric power until October 2, 1962, and then with diesel power.

The road shared a station in downtown Galt with the Lake Erie and Northern, and in addition operated into the CPR station on a spur line in order to provide connections to Kitchener for all main line trains. By 1895 through tickets were issued to points on the line in conjunction with the CPR. The operations were co-ordinated with those of the LE&N after the latter was built, with substantial interchange of equipment after the GR's voltage was raised to 1,500 in 1921. Service on the Hespeler line was provided in later years almost exclusively by two combines built for the LE&N in 1915.

This was the most profitable of all Canadian interurbans, yielding 8 to 10 per cent on investment for a number of years. Prior to 1930, in only one year, 1921, did it fail to cover interest. After 1931 its accounts were consolidated with those of the LE&N. In the thirty-two years prior to this consolidation, a rate of return of over 5 per cent was earned in twenty-five of the years.

*Lake Erie and Northern Railway Company*[17]

The other CPR line in the Grand Valley was the Lake Erie and Northern, which by contrast was one of the last electric lines built. It was incorporated by Brantford business men, including farm-implement manufacturer H. Cockshutt, in 1911 to build a steam road south to the lake as an additional freight outlet for Brantford industries. The Canadian Pacific became interested in the line as a feeder, purchased control, leased it for 999 years, and completed it southward to Port Dover and northward to a connection with its own line and the GR at Galt. The lines from Brantford to Galt and from Waterford to Simcoe were built in 1914, and the two missing links, from Brantford to Waterford and Simcoe to Port Dover, in 1915, with steam operation. At this time the city of Brantford was interested in electrification of the line, and an agreement was finally reached whereby the CPR agreed to electrify the route and to buy from the city the portion of the derelict Grand Valley Railway from Paris to Galt. The city was anxious to get this off its hands yet preserve electric train service to Galt. Electrification of the line from Brantford to Galt was completed late in 1915 and opened for passenger service on February 7, 1916, thus permitting Brantford to abandon service on the GV north of Paris, action which by then was imperative because the track was in such bad shape that cars could scarcely be kept on it. The LE&N had paralleled the GV track almost in its entirety, except in Paris, where it stayed on the upper level, whereas the GV descended to the lower.

Electrification was pushed southward, so that through electric service was opened to Simcoe on May 30, 1916, and to Port Dover on July 22 of the same year. A 1,500-volt DC system was employed with trolley rather than pantograph. Eight cars were built for the line by the Preston Car and Coach Company—four 59-foot passenger motor cars of seventy-passenger capacity, two trailers, and two combines. All had clerestory roofs and, curiously, wooden sides over steel sheeting. The cars, which weighed over 80,000 pounds, were powered with four 85-horsepower Westinghouse motors. Typically trains were operated on two-hour schedules. Heavy construction was employed on the line, which was well maintained throughout. A union station was erected at Colborne and Water streets in Brantford, in conjunction with the Brantford and Hamilton. Unlike the GV, which used street car tracks, the LE&N reached downtown Brantford on its own private right of way near the river.

Freight revenues were important from the beginning, but less so than on the GR, and not until 1928 did they constitute more than half of gross revenue. Passenger revenue reached its peak of 609,000 in 1921, and fell steadily thereafter; the 1931 figure was only 231,000. The road never suffered an operating deficit prior to 1932, but likewise never earned as much as 5 per cent on investment or enough to cover its interest. With a relatively high investment per mile, the volume of traffic was inadequate to allow a reasonable return, even before significant development of the automobile.

After the end of World War II, the cars were renovated. Nevertheless, passenger business fell, and in 1950 and 1952 application was made to discontinue all passenger service. The Board of Transport Commissioners denied the petition as a result of the protests of the cities. The commissioners took the position that, although the passenger service might be unprofitable, the decision must be made in terms of the profit status of the road as a whole. Traffic continued to decline, however, and in 1955 application was renewed and this time granted. Passengers carried on the GV and the LE&N had fallen from 2 million in 1920 (and 1.7 million in 1944) to 160,000 in 1954. All passenger service ended on April, 24 1955. Up to the end, however, equipment and track were kept in first-class condition. A substantial portion of the passengers in later years consisted of high school students from Port Dover transported to and from the high school in Simcoe. The road, incidentally, did a substantial express business at Easter time in cut flowers from the Port Dover area. Electric freight operation was retained until 1963, when diesel power was introduced. The Simcoe–Port Dover portion has been abandoned.

As noted, after 1931, the financial accounts were consolidated with those of the GR. Freight traffic on the two roads continued to rise, and in 1953 was more than twice the 1929 figure. Nevertheless, the road encountered difficulties in meeting operating expenses after 1946, as costs rose faster than revenues. However, elimination of passenger service brought substantial improvement; this service was obviously suffering an out-of-pocket loss. In the twenty-four years of combined accounts with the GR down through 1955, deficits were incurred in thirteen years, including every year after 1945 except 1952 and 1955, and never did the return exceed 5 per cent. However, the roads were important freight feeders for the parent line.

### Grand Valley Railway Company[18]

The Grand Valley was one of the most unsuccessful of the Ontario lines, its experience demonstrating clearly that, even in the days of relative prosperity for the interurbans, a line connecting relatively small cities some distance apart, with virtually no freight business, could not succeed.

The GV was promoted by the Von Echa Company, a somewhat mysterious organization incorporated in West Virginia, with the centre of its activities in Harrisburg, Pennsylvania. How the company became interested in the Grand Valley–London area is unknown, but shortly after 1900 it developed a plan for a system connecting Brantford and Galt with London, and, ultimately, with Toronto and Detroit. It acquired and completed the Brantford Street Railway, and in 1904 built eight miles of line from Brantford to Paris, service commencing on May 22, 1904. The additional thirteen miles of track from Paris to Galt, on the east side of the Grand River, were completed late in 1904 and cars operated to the Galt boundary. A line from Blue Lake to St. George was started but never finished. After long discussions, agreement was finally reached with the city of Galt for operation commencing on October 6, 1905, into the downtown area over tracks of the Galt, Preston and Hespler. As one concession the company agreed not to operate its cars on Sunday into Galt, a centre of the anti-Sunday-activity movement. This Brantford–Galt line was built primarily on a private right of way, but to relatively low standards, with substantial grades. Downtown Brantford was reached via street railway tracks. The Paris station was on the lower level, east of the river.

In 1906 control of the road passed from the Von Echa Company to a group headed by A. J. Pattison of Toronto, and in 1907 together with the Brantford Street Railway and the Woodstock–Ingersoll line to the M. A. Vernor interests of Pittsburgh. Some reconstruction was done by the new owners, but operation was not profitable, and in 1908 the company suffered an operating loss. In 1909 control of the three companies was acquired by the G. B. Woods group of Toronto. Between 1904 and 1908, when other electric lines were prospering, the GV experienced almost no growth in traffic. In 1911 the company fell into receivership and by 1912 the line had deteriorated so badly that a snowstorm in February brought all operations to a halt.

Service was resumed as far as Paris in March, but the remainder of the line to Galt was in such bad shape that operation was unsafe. Only the less unprofitable Brantford city routes kept the company afloat at all. In 1913 bondholder groups brought suit against the directors for misuse of funds, and the city of Brantford instituted legal action to compel the meeting of franchise obligations relating to paving, and payment of back taxes, threatening cancellation of the franchise. In 1914, both the city of Brantford and the Lake Erie and Northern offered to buy the line (together with the Brantford city system); the city offer was higher and was accepted after approval by the voters on March 23, 1914. Brantford thus paid $253,000 for the city and inter-urban lines and assumed liability for $125,000 of outstanding bonds, owned by Canadian General Electric, and on December 19, 1914, took over operations. The city lines and the Brantford–Paris portion of the interurban were rebuilt, and the segment north of Paris was repaired just enough to allow limited operation. In 1915 the city reached an agreement with the LE&N whereby the latter bought the Paris–Galt portion for $30,000. A short segment in Galt was retained for freight switching, the remainder being abandoned in 1916. The LE&N acquired the line in order to eliminate two crossovers as well as potential competition, and the city of Brantford was glad to get rid of a white elephant. The city continued to operate the Brantford–Paris line, essentially as an extension of the street railway system, in competition with the LE&N. Gradual decline in business led several times to consideration of abandonment before the final action was taken in 1929.[19]

The over-all financial history of the GV was curious: the enterprise as a whole never earned even a reasonably adequate return except in two years (1909 and 1910); yet it had a remarkable ability, through all sorts of adversity, to avoid showing an operating deficit (except in 1908). This situation reflected partly the slightly better earnings of the Brantford city lines (which were combined with the intercity line for most of the period), and partly the gross neglect of maintenance, which soon placed the road in the position that it could not continue to operate.

### Woodstock, Thames Valley and Ingersoll Electric Railway Company

The Woodstock, Thames Valley and Ingersoll was the smallest of the Ontario interurbans; intended as a link in a through line from Toronto and Hamilton to London, it never became more than a strictly local operation connecting two relatively small towns. The line together with the Grand Valley with which it was to connect, was promoted by the Von Echa Company and managed by Dr. S. Ritter Ickes, who represented the Von Echa group in Ontario. The charter was obtained in 1900, and on November 8, 1900, service was opened from Woodstock to Beachville. The following year the entire ten-mile line to Ingersoll was brought into service. The subsequent corporate history was the same as that of the GV until the latter was acquired by the city of Brantford. At this point the owners abandoned the WTV&I line to the bondholders, who took control in 1915 and operated it for a decade. Even after bus competition was established in 1922, the little road managed to cover operating expenses until 1925, when it was abandoned. The total annual receipts throughout the life of the road were only about $25,000 or $2,500 a mile. Two cars were normally operated, meeting at Beachville. The entire line was built on the edge of the highway from Woodstock to Ingersoll on the south side of the river, except the last mile into Woodstock, which was diverted over side streets.

### THE TORONTO AREA ROADS

The radial network around Toronto, with 137 miles of line, was much more limited than might be expected, especially in comparison to the systems operating out of Cleveland, Detroit, Columbus, Toledo, Cincinnati, and other cities. The lines that were built around Toronto all suffered from the lack of an entrance into the downtown area. It is difficult to explain the limited development, except to some extent in terms of the domination of the transportation picture in the area by Sir William Mackenzie, who was interested in so many things that he had relatively little time or money for electric railroads. The relatively bad relations between Mackenzie and the city of Toronto also played a part.

### Toronto and York Radial Railway Company

The largest of the Toronto roads was the Toronto and York Radial Railway, made up of three disconnected lines. The longest was the Metropolitan division, extending forty-eight miles from Toronto to Sutton near Lake Simcoe. The other two, which were essentially suburban operations, extended from the Humber River in Toronto to Port Credit, and from Woodbine to West Hill beyond Scarborough. The history of these lines is a very complicated one, and can be sketched only briefly.

The Metropolitan Street Railway Company was incorporated in 1877, and was gradually extended, as a horse-car line, up Yonge Street to Eglinton (1885). In 1889 the line was electrified and in 1890 reached York Mills. An extension to Richmond Hill went into operation in 1896, replacing a stage coach line, on April 14, 1899, the section from Richmond Hill to Newmarket was opened. The enterprise had now grown beyond a mere suburban operation. Control was acquired by the Mackenzie interests, and in 1904 the road became a part of the Toronto and York Radial Railway Company (chartered in 1898), whose stock was held by the city system, Toronto

Railway Company, also a Mackenzie property. Shortly thereafter plans for extension were developed, and on June 1, 1907, a high-speed private right-of-way line was opened from Newmarket to Jackson's Point on Lake Simcoe. In 1909 the line was extended two miles into Sutton.

The Metropolitan line had one branch, the Schomberg and Aurora Railroad. This company was chartered in 1896, and commenced construction in 1901 from a connection with the Grand Trunk at Bond Lake, two miles south of Aurora. The fourteen-mile line into Schomberg was completed in 1904 and operated as a steam road. It had meanwhile passed into Mackenzie hands, and was absorbed into T&YR in 1904, and extended to connect with the latter's line. But it was not electrified until 1916. Some cars then operated through to Toronto, but most made connections at Bond Lake. Steam road freight cars were handled.

The Metropolitan line never reached downtown Toronto. Originally, it terminated at the Canadian Pacific crossing north of Bloor Street where passengers transferred to city cars. In 1915 the city required the company to cut its line back to Farnham Avenue, and for several months the gap had no service, passengers being forced to walk the five intervening blocks while the city carried on a bitter and senseless fight with Mackenzie. From Farnham Avenue the line operated on Yonge Street (for the most part on the edge of the right of way) to Aurora, perfectly straight except for a few short stretches, but with grades up to 8 per cent. The private right of way paralleled the highway to a point south of Newmarket, where it swung eastward, arcing around to Queensville, and thence in another gradual arc westward to Keswick. From Orchard Beach the line paralleled the lake (far enough back to permit cottages to be built on the shore) in a half moon to Jackson's Point, and then ran straight south to Sutton. The primary traffic of the line was of two types, the suburban service from Richmond Hill and intermediate points, and the heavy seasonal traffic to Lake Simcoe points. To a whole generation of Torontonians, the most favoured summer week-end trip was one on the Metropolitan to Lake Simcoe. A considerable volume of freight business developed, primarily carload interchange business with the CNR, and yielded from 10 to 15 per cent of revenue for many years. Substantial milk traffic was handled, and trainloads of ice from Lake Simcoe. The track was standard gauge, and thus operation on street railway tracks in Toronto was not possible.

The line (together with the Scarborough and Mimico lines noted below) experienced a phenomenal growth in passenger traffic over the years, from 350,000 in 1900 and 2,240,000 in 1905 to a peak of 11,689,000 in 1921. For many years it had the greatest volume of any intercity electric road in Canada—although much of this was of a very short distance suburban variety. The return on investment was very good up until the period around 1920. In all but one of the twenty-two years after 1900 the return exceeded 5 per cent, and was over 10 per cent in eight of these. Despite the continued growth in traffic, very little change occurred in equipment or line after 1912, expansion and improvement being delayed by the uncertainty over Hydro radial plans. The old cars became increasingly obsolete and deteriorated.

Finally, the city of Toronto acquired the Toronto Railway Company from the Mackenzie interests, and in 1920, in the so-called "clean-up deal," purchased the T&YR along with the other Mackenzie properties in the area. The voters approved the action on January 1, 1921. However, a year and a half of negotiations followed before the city actually took possession on August 16, 1922. The city paid $2,375,000 for the three portions of T&YR outside the city, and $585,000 for those in the city. The city portions were incorporated into the Toronto Transportation Commission system, and the line on Yonge relaid as a double-track line in the centre of the street to replace the old single-track line on the west edge. TTC cars commenced to operate to the city limits at Deloraine Avenue on November 2, 1922. The portions outside of the city were turned over to Ontario Hydro for operation under contract, and designated as the Hydro-Electric Railways, Toronto and York Division. Substantial sums were spent on improvements, but no over-all reconstruction was undertaken.

The financial results under Hydro operation were not happy, as a sharp decline in traffic after 1922 converted a $200,000 a year operating profit into an operating deficit, leaving the city burdened in addition with interest on $4 million of debentures. Extensive discussion between the city and Hydro resulted in the termination of the contract with Hydro, and the city took over operation of the lines on January 12, 1927. The Mimico and Scarborough lines were permanently incorporated into the TTC, but the Metropolitan line was retained by the city, as such, operations being carried on by TTC as an agent. The entire Metropolitan line was widened to the 4-foot 10⅝-inch gauge of the city system in order to permit operation of cars through to the downtown area, but in practice this plan was never carried out except for express cars which for a time operated through at night to Yonge and Front. The gauge change brought to an end all carload freight operation and bitter complaints from a factory in Aurora which had no other rail connections. As a consequence, a mile of standard gauge line paralleling the main track was retained in Aurora. A third rail could not be used because it was impossible to lay two rails in the space of just over two inches provided by the variation in gauges. Because of continued losses, the Schomberg branch was abandoned by the city on June 20, 1927.[20] The action brought notice from the federal government that the city had violated the original Dominion subsidy agreement, which called for operation of at least two trains a day as a condition for obtaining the subsidy. The city flatly rejected the argument, and the Dominion did not press the case.

The city had hoped that TTC operation would improve financial results by cutting overhead, but this goal was not realized, and further declines in traffic brought continued operating losses to the extent of $97,000 in 1928. In not a single year after municipal operations commenced in 1927 were operating expenses covered. In 1929 the number of runs was cut in half, and co-ordinated bus service instituted as far as Newmarket. In June 1929 the TTC recommended abandonment, on the basis of a report by R. M. Feustel of Indiana Service Company. The towns served strongly opposed abandonment, insisting that Toronto was obligated to continue to supply the service, but a year of negotiations over the question of sharing of deficits with the various towns and of postponement of abandonment brought no results, and on March 16, 1930, service came to an end. However the municipalities between Toronto and Richmond Hill arranged for resumption of service as far as the latter town by purchasing the line for $66,000 and agreeing to meet deficits, and the cars commenced to roll again on the ten-mile segment on July 17, 1930. Lightweight cars built by the Ottawa Car Company for the Mimico line were used. Similar negotiations with the towns between Richmond Hill and Newmarket broke down, and the remainder of the line was dismantled. The Richmond Hill segment was operated successfully until October 10, 1948, when all service was permanently discontinued and replaced by buses, largely because the track was worn out and the volume of traffic did not warrant replacement. The city route on Yonge to the city limits was abandoned in 1954 when the subway was built. The subway parallels the original Metropolitan line from the CPR crossing to Eglinton, and bus service extends from Eglinton to the city limits.

The Metropolitan venture had been a very costly one for Toronto; in addition to the original capital cost of over $2 million, the city had to make good more than $2 million in deficits, and managed to realize only about $430,000 in salvage value. The net cost to the city, including interest, was about $7 million, in exchange for which it obtained nothing but ill will from neighbouring communities. City purchase coincided exactly with the very sharp drop in business due to the rise of the automobile; few electric lines ever changed so quickly from a prosperous condition to one of hopeless unprofitability.

The other two lines of the T&YR were essentially suburban street car lines.[21] The Port Credit line was incorporated as the Toronto and Mimico Railway and Light Company in 1890. The portion from Sunnyside to the Humber River was placed in service in 1892, and the line extended to Mimico Creek the following year. Little double-deck open cars were used, the traffic being largely confined to summer sightseeing. The company was absorbed by Toronto Railway in 1893, and extended to Long Branch, service from Sunnyside opening on July 1, 1894. This was primarily a summer route in earlier years, reaching summer cottages and resorts along the shore. In 1905 track was extended to Port Credit, and the line surveyed to Oakville, but no further construction was undertaken. In 1906 two ninety-six-passenger open cars built by Toronto Railway were placed in summer service. These were among the largest electric cars ever employed.

In 1904 the road was taken over by Metropolitan and its operations divorced from Toronto Railway; although both were Mackenzie enterprises, it was considered preferable to keep the suburban operations separate. Thus, as a part of T&YR, the line was acquired by the city of Toronto as of 1922, and turned over to Hydro for operation. The gauge was reduced to 4 feet 8½ inches and new cars obtained. The line was taken back by the city in 1927, and the following year merged into the TTC. The gauge was changed back to 4 feet 10⅞ inches, and the line double tracked (in 1928), rebuilt as far as Mimico, and operated with city equipment. The three miles from Long Branch to Port Credit were separately operated as a side-of-the-road rural trolley until abandonment in 1935. The Long Branch portion is still operated in 1965, but now serves a highly urbanized area essentially as a street car line.

The Scarborough line was started by the Toronto and Scarboro' Electric Railway, Light and Power Company, incorporated in 1892. Street car service to Victoria Park from Kingston Road and Queen Street commenced in 1893, the track laid on the north side of Kingston Road. The line reached Half Way House on July 12, 1901, and West Hill, in Scarborough township, in 1905. The line was absorbed by Toronto Railway in 1895, and then divorced from it and turned over to Metropolitan (T&YR) in 1904. Thus it passed to the city in 1922, and was operated by Hydro until 1927, except for the section from Queen to Victoria Park which was incorporated into the Kingston Road line of TTC. In 1927, the line was taken over by the city, and merged into TTC, the city operation being extended to Birchmont. The radial line was abandoned on June 25, 1936, and the city line cut back to Victoria Park in 1955. The gauge of this line was always 4 feet 10⅞ inches.

## Toronto Suburban Railway Company[22]

The other Toronto electric line had a peculiar and not altogether happy history. For most of the years of its life it was only a suburban street car line. When construction of the major intercity line commenced, it proceeded at a snail's pace, and was not finished until the industry was on the downhill path. As a consequence, the extension ruined the company financially.

The enterprise was incorporated in 1894 as the Toronto Suburban Street Railway Company and built in the mid-nineties from Keele and Dundas streets in Toronto via Dundas Road to Lambton Mills, and to Weston via Keele and Weston Road. In addition, a street car line was built from Bathurst Street and Davenport Road via Davenport and Weston roads to Keele. The line was promoted by A. H. Royce of Toronto, a prominent financial and social leader of the community. Around 1901 the line developed great ambitions of building to Hamilton, but the project never got beyond the survey stage, and the company continued for a decade as a small suburban carrier, with about ten miles of line and a moderate rate of return on investment.

In 1911 the line was acquired by Mackenzie, and plans for extension were revived, this time in the direction of Guelph. First, however, the Weston line was extended in a crooked winding route into Woodbridge, following the road for a distance and thence the Humber River. The track reached Woodbridge in 1913, but a dispute with the town over location prevented introduction of regular service until October 10, 1914. The main line to Guelph was surveyed in 1911, and construction commenced in 1912. Much of the grading was finished in 1913 except for heavy work near Lambton. Work continued in 1914, during which year most of the rail was laid. The war slowed down construction, and not until April 14, 1917, was service inaugurated on the forty-nine-mile line from Lambton to Guelph.

The road was built to relatively high standards, with substantial grading and filling and several extensive bridges and trestles, including a 711-foot steel bridge over the Humber and a 315-foot wooden trestle across the west branch of the Credit River. The track was nearly all on a private right of way, following Dundas Street to Summerville and then cutting cross country via Meadowvale, Huttonville, Norval, Georgetown, Acton, and Eden Mills, south of the Grand Trunk's old main line. The line climbed 755 feet from Lambton to a point west of Acton. The operation was 1,500-volt DC with catenary overhead, and the track, unlike the old line of the company, was standard gauge. In 1916 the company sought permission to change a portion of its Toronto trackage to standard to allow through operation. Although the city strongly opposed on the grounds that operation of interurban cars on city streets was unsafe, the permission was granted and the changes made. The interurban cars then terminated at Keele and Dundas, still a long distance from downtown. The delays which had plagued construction were not over, even as the introduction of regular service approached; several of the cars completed for the company by the Preston Car and Coach Company were destroyed when a fire swept the car building plants, so TS was forced to restrict its operations to a limited scale for several months. The 59-foot, sixty-two-passenger cars were of the centre door type, unique in Canadian interurban operation. Two 61-foot-9-inch cars were built for the line by the Niagara, St. Catharines and Toronto Railway in 1924.[23]

The line was scarcely finished before the road's parent company, the Canadian Northern, was acquired by the Dominion government to become a portion of Canadian National Railways. The attitude of the latter towards TS shifted several times over the next decade. At first the CNR was willing to let the road go to become a part of the Hydro radial system, but when the plans for the latter fell through Sir Henry Thornton became enthusiastic for a time about a system of electric lines in the Toronto area under CNR ownership. He merged the TS with the unfinished Toronto Eastern, commenced to complete the latter, and refused a 1922 offer of the city of Toronto to buy the TS in its entirety. The line was operated, after 1923, as Canadian National Electric Railways, Toronto Suburban District. In 1924 and 1925 a new entrance into the city was built from west of Lambton to St. Clair and Keele via a private right of way with an underpass under the CPR. Plans were developed to bring the cars downtown to the Union Station over main line CNR tracks. The old Lambton line was sold to the township and operated by the TTC till its abandonment in 1928. Meanwhile, in 1923, upon expiration of the franchise, the city routes of the TS were purchased by the city, as of November 24, rehabilitated, and incorporated into the TTC. The Weston line was sold to Weston and York Township in 1925 and operated for them by the TTC until September 13, 1948. Because the line had been subject to extensive bus competition, the CNR was glad to dispose of it; once the municipalities took it over, bus competition was eliminated. Shortly after the sale, the CNR abandoned the Weston–Woodbridge line on May 10, 1926.

The very moderate earnings of the early years had improved slowly to a relatively high rate of return by 1911. But then came the heavy investment in the extension, the long delay in getting operations under way, and the development of the automobile. The rate of return ranged from one to 3 per cent from 1912 through 1920, and in most of the period did not cover interest. Operating deficits appeared in 1921, and grew steadily; revenues fell while expenses continued to rise. The operating ratio was 145 by 1925. Thus the TS was by far the most unprofitable electric line in Canada in this period. After 1926 some reduction in expenses occurred, but substantial operating deficits were incurred each year from 1923 on. Under private ownership operations would have stopped by the mid-twenties, but pressures on the government to keep the road going resulted in continued deficit operation when there was no chance of improvement. By 1931, only 300 passengers a day were being carried, and, finally, all operations were discontinued on August 1 of that year. The CNR allowed the bond interest to go into default in 1931, taking the position (strongly protested by the bondholders) that it had no obligation to meet the payments. About $500,000 was obtained from salvage (including the sale of the Weston line), and the bondholders received 25 cents on the dollar. Most of the equipment that the CNR owned was sent to the Niagara, St. Catharines and Toronto. Car no. 107, which made the last run on TS, made the mornihg trips on the Niagara–St. Catharines road (as car no. 83) the day passenger service was ended in March 1959.

The line's extension to Guelph was a major error: placed in service when automobiles were already becoming common, it was hopelessly unprofitable from the beginning. In the years between 1921 and 1931, the total operating deficit accumulated was $646,000, and bond interest payments amounted to $1,215,000. Clearly the road should have been abandoned at least six years before it actually was.

### THE NIAGARA ROADS

There were two systems in the Niagara peninsula, the Niagara, St. Catharines and Toronto, and the Niagara Falls Park and River.

### *Niagara, St. Catharines and Toronto Railway Company*[24]

This road was one of the largest (with seventy-five miles of line at the peak) and most successful of all Canadian intercity electric lines. One of its predecessor companies

G

operated the first intercity electric line in Canada, and the road was the last to operate intercity electric passenger service in the country. Unlike the other lines, the NStC&T operated a network of routes, rather than one or two single ones. None of these were very long, but in total they constituted a significant system.

The NStC&T was developed in the period around 1900 by the Haines syndicate, which had its headquarters in New York but included several Canadians, notably Toronto banker Aemilius Jarvis. The company (chartered in 1898) took over the old St. Catharines and Niagara Central, a steam road opened in 1888 between the two cities of its title. This road had never developed adequate traffic, and was in bankruptcy by 1899. Under the NStC&T the road was improved and electrified, and electric passenger service established on July 19, 1900, between St. Catharines and Niagara Falls, Ontario, on what was always regarded as the company's main line. The route entered Niagara Falls on the track of a local line, the Niagara Falls, Wesley Park and Clifton (absorbed by the NStC&T), and terminated at the foot of Bridge Street. Later arrangements were made to run the cars across the upper steel bridge on the tracks of the International Railway Company to Niagara Falls, New York. In St. Catharines the line extended from the station on St. Paul Street opposite Mary Street along several streets and thence onto a private right of way along the old canal. It stayed on high ground past Merritton, with the help of a half-mile wooden trestle, and continued on a private right of way through Thorold. Power was obtained originally from the Falls plant of Niagara Power Company, later from Ontario Hydro.

In 1901 the NStC&T completed and placed in service a four-mile line from St. Catharines to Port Dalhousie. Cars operated on the main line to Lake Street, thence on a private right of way on the east bank of the Welland Canal, across the canal, through Port Dalhousie, and terminated at the wharf. In the summer some cars operated directly from Port Dalhousie to Niagara Falls without going into downtown St. Catharines. Two sidewheeler steamers, the *Lakeside* and the *Garden City*, were purchased from their independent operators, and combined boat-rail service from Toronto to Niagara was established. The Dalhousie City and the Northumberland were added at a later date. Service was operated from Buffalo to Toronto in conjunction with the International Railway's Niagara–Buffalo line and the steamers, a $3\frac{1}{2}$-hour trip, at a fare of $1.50 round trip. The steamers operated until 1947, providing a very inexpensive and popular outing from Toronto, and a major source of revenue for the line.

On May 1, 1901, the NStC&T purchased the Port Dalhousie, St. Catharines and Thorold, the oldest intercity electric line in Canada. In 1877, a horse-car line had been built by the St. Catharines Street Railway Company from St. Catharines to Merritton and Thorold, on Queenston Street and Thorold Road and along the bank of the old canal to Thorold. The road was reorganized in 1882 as the St. Catharines, Merritton and Thorold Street Railway Company.

The line was difficult to operate, and the steep grades on what was an unusually long route for a horse-car line were hard on the horses. In May, 1887, President E. A. Smyth notified the *Street Railway Journal* that he was going to electrify the line. A contract was made with the Van Depoele Company, trolley wire was strung up in August; a water-driven dynamo was set up by the Welland Canal; and Van Depoele 15-horsepower motors were installed on the horse cars. On October 5 the first electric car ventured out onto the track. But this first run was not without mishap; the car came onto the sharp unbanked curves so rapidly that it went flying off on several occasions. Also, it was unable to negotiate the steepest grade. However, after some relocation of track on the curves and readjustments of the running gear of the cars, they were soon providing regular service, and the horses were sold. By December the company reported that the operation was far more reliable than the horses, and claimed the line to be the world's longest electric line. Three more motors designed especially for the heavy grades were ordered in January 1888. The company reported that the business increased 35 per cent (with the same track) and costs were reduced

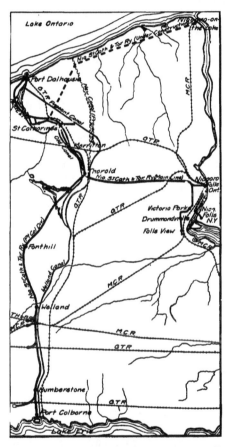

FIGURE 8. Niagara, St. Catharines and Toronto Railway, 1913. The Niagara-on-the-Lake line was under construction at the time. The Grand Trunk line shown from Merritton to Port Dalhousie was later taken over and electrified. (From *Canadian Railway and Marine World*, July 1913, p. 339.)

$18 a day as a result of electrification. In February 1888 President Smyth indicated in a letter to the *Street Railway Journal* that he was very well satisfied. By December the road had ten cars in operation. One experiment was unsuccessful, namely, the use of the two-trolley-wire troller system. The troller did not stay on the wires satisfactorily, and the company turned to the use of a single trolley wire and underrunning trolley wheel, and bonded the rail joints for rail return of current. For the next twenty years operations continued largely unchanged. The company was reorganized as the Port Dalhousie, St. Catharines and Thorold Electric Street Railway in 1893, and continued to keep separate accounts for some years after absorption by the NStC&T. The latter's main line more or less paralleled the old line from St. Catharines to Thorold, but at a higher and more uniform grade, and crossed it three times. Local service continued on the original line following absorption, and was extended to the McKinnon factory on the west edge of St. Catharines.

In 1905 the American interest in the NStC&T was purchased by the F. Nicholls–E. R. Woods group in Toronto and their financial allies, the Mackenzie-Mann interests. Nicholls was president of Canadian General Electric and vice-president of Toronto Railway. Thus the road became an associate of the Mackenzie properties, and in 1908 control was acquired directly by the Mackenzie-Mann Company and ultimately turned over to the Canadian Northern Railway. Under the new ownership expansion and modernization of the road was undertaken. A new line was built southward from Thorold to Welland in 1907 and extended to Port Colborne in 1911. This was a private-right-of-way route, cars connecting at Thorold with Niagara trains, and providing Welland with connections to CNR mainline trains. In 1913, a twelve-mile line was built from St. Catharines northeastward to Niagara-on-the-Lake, about half on the highway allowance, half on a private right of way. Around 1905, the Mackenzie interests promoted the Toronto and Hamilton Railway to be built as a high-speed route from Toronto to a connection with the NStC&T at St. Catharines, and although surveys were made nothing ever came of the project. The NStC&T was also included in Sir Adam Beck's planned radial network a decade later.

This was in its entirety a 600-volt DC system. Passenger service was very frequent. Service from St. Catharines to Niagara Falls, Niagara-on-the-Lake, and Port Colborne was typically hourly (with hour and a half intervals to Port Colborne during a part of the day), and every thirty minutes to Port Dalhousie as well as on the Merritton local line. A variety of equipment was employed; there were a number of 50-foot monitor roof wooden cars acquired at the time of modernization, and smaller cars for the lighter traffic lines. In 1915 the road acquired six 55-foot semi-steel cars from Preston Car Company, with weight of 75,000 and capacity of sixty-seven passengers.

The line was typically more profitable than the industry as a whole. Passenger traffic grew rapidly from 254,000 in 1902 to 4,687,000 in 1914, and to 8,365,000 in the peak year, 1921. These figures include local passengers on the street car lines in St. Catharines. The rate of return was not spectacular prior to 1910, but for the next decade it ranged from 7 to 11 per cent. One of the factors in the prosperity was the growth of freight traffic, for which the road had been designed initially; in 1913 there were sixty industrial and other sidings, and a heavy carload freight traffic handled by electric locomotives. In 1902, 79,000 tons were handled; in 1918, 430,000.

In 1917–18, the government acquired the road along with its parent, Canadian Northern, but made few changes in operations. The government indicated a willingness to sell the line to the municipalities, and almost all of the latter approved purchase by popular vote in 1922. But a few opposed, and no action was taken. Then Sir Henry Thornton became interested in expansion of the interurban lines and in 1923 commenced his major programme of improvements. New stations were built, including an extensive modern station in St. Catherines between Balfour Street and Welland Avenue facing Geneva Street.[25] Track was reconstructed and new equipment purchased. The CNR's Merritton–Port Dalhousie branch was turned over to the

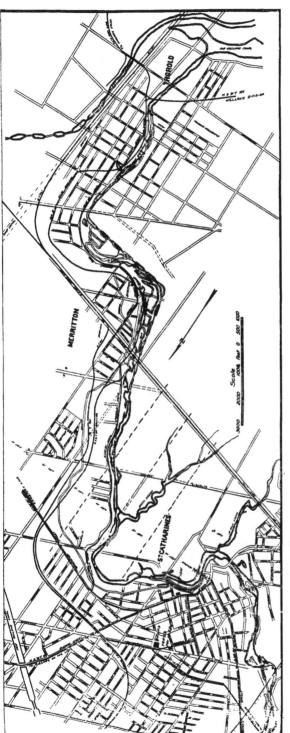

FIGURE 9. Niagara, St. Catharines and Toronto Railway local lines in St. Catharines, Merritton, and Thorold, 1913. The station was subsequently relocated and rebuilt. Some trackage was built after this map was drawn. (From *Canadian Railway and Marine World*, July 1913, p. 338.)

line and electrified with catenary overhead to give a new high-speed route to supplement the old line. This was known as the Grantham Subdivision. There were now three lines from Merritton to St. Catharines. But the "low line" was a purely local line and the Grantham Subdivision line served only the CNR Merritton station. After 1922 the road was usually designated as the Canadian National Electric Railways, NStC&T Railway District, and the cars labelled in this fashion. The original name was kept for some legal purposes, however.

After 1920, passenger traffic fell somewhat, but the loss down to 1929 was only 25 per cent, less than the industry as a whole. Freight traffic continued to rise, the 1926 peak being 75 per cent greater than the earlier peak in 1918. The rate of return was good up through 1923, but fell sharply in 1924 as a result of the substantial investment in modernization; never again was it to recover. Nevertheless, the road covered interest in every year prior to 1930, an extremely good record in the electric railway industry.

The depression hit the road very hard. Freight and passenger traffic fell sharply, and small operating deficits were incurred in 1933 and 1934. Retrenchment in operations soon commenced. In 1931, the Niagara-on-the-Lake line service was discontinued and the track cut back to Port Weller. The old local line from Thorold to St. Catharines was torn up in 1931 (operation ending June 1) when the town of Merritton refused to renew the franchise and won out in a legal battle.[26] In 1940 passenger service on the main line from St. Catharines to Niagara was discontinued, but was restored in 1942 at government request as a war-time measure. The line was finally abandoned September 14, 1947. Freight traffic rose substantially as recovery from the depression came, and in 1937 reached an all-time high. The total remained remarkably stable down through 1951; in that year it was 50 per cent greater than in 1916, for example. As truck competition increased, the volume fell in the mid-fifties. Passenger traffic, which had nearly reached old-time highs during World War II, fell drastically after the war, dropping from over 6 million in 1945 to 1,100,000 in 1945, and to 224,000 in 1955. By the early fifties operating expenses were barely covered.

Service from Thorold to St. Catharines via the high line ceased in 1947 at the same time as the main line service. On March 1, 1950, regular passenger service ended from St. Catharines to Port Dalhousie, leaving only the Thorold–Port Colborne line in regular passenger service. Despite constant rumours, the line was operated until March 1959, usually on a two-hour schedule. In 1956 it was sent the Windsor, Essex and Lake Shore cars that had been in use on the Montreal and Southern Counties, to supplement its older equipment. This line was the last really typical intercity passenger service in operation in either the United States or Canada; other services, such as those out of Quebec City and Chicago, were essentially suburban operations.

In total, the road provided electric passenger service for fifty-four years. Freight service was continued with electric power until 1960, when the line was dieselized. The road earned a return in excess of 5 per cent in fifteen years, and suffered an operating deficit (after taxes) in eighteen.

### Niagara Falls Park and River Railway Company[27]

On May 24, 1893, the twelve-mile line of the Niagara Falls Park and River was placed in operation between Chippawa and Queenston, via Niagara Falls, paralleling the Niagara River. The original southern terminus was at Chippawa on the Niagara River above the Horseshoe Falls. The line followed the river past the upper rapids,

Horseshoe Falls, and the two bridges, ran above Whirlpool Rapids and up on to Queenston Heights, and then descended by a series of spiralling loops to the wharves at Queenston. It was of course primarily a sightseeing road, and ran normally from May 24 to October 30. The company had been formed in 1891, and in September 1892 was given, by the Niagara Parks Commission, a forty-year contract to operate the road on park property.

Originally the line connected at Chippawa with a ferry for Buffalo, but in the late nineties it commenced to operate over the bridge of the International Railway at Niagara Falls, into Niagara Falls, New York. In 1899 a suspension bridge primarily for trolley operation was built at Queenston and opened for service on July 21. Arrangements were made with the independent Niagara Gorge Railway for loop operation. Commencing from Niagara Falls, New York, the cars went north down the river on the tracks of the Niagara Gorge line (which descended to the floor of the river at Whirlpool Rapids), crossed the Queenston bridge, came down the Canadian side, and passed back across the Niagara bridge, Connections were also made with Toronto steamers at the Queenston wharf. Stopovers between cars were allowed for sightseeing and picnics. For the next thirty years this was without question the most popular trolley sightseeing trip in the two countries. Half-hourly service, with additional cars in peak periods, was typical.

Initially promoted by Toronto capital and such distinguished men as Sir William Van Horne of the CPR and James Ross of Montreal Street Railways, the road soon passed into the hands of the International Railway Company of Buffalo, and it was operated after 1901 as the Canadian division of International.

The road had a surprising amount of rolling stock in the nineties; in 1893, it purchased ten 28-foot closed cars, ten 28-foot open motor cars, three 18-foot closed cars, and twelve 18-foot open trailers. They were built by Patterson and Corbin of St. Catharines, the motor cars having two 25-horsepower Canadian General Electric motors built in Peterborough, and McGuire truck assemblies. The electrical installation was Thompson–Houston, the power supplied originally by NFP&R's own hydro-electric plant, plus a supplementary steam plant for power for the Queenston grade.

Traffic grew slowly from 1894 to 1901, jumped greatly in 1902, and then remained relatively constant down to 1926, although there was considerable year-to-year variation. This pattern was very different from the usual electric line, largely because, unlike the usual passenger flow, the summer tourist travel to Niagara was affected by a variety of forces such as weather conditions. Except in 1915, when damages from the accident noted below caused losses, the road was relatively profitable up to 1922, but never thereafter covered operating expenses except in 1925. Freight traffic was negligible except for a few years when hydro-electric plants were being built along this line.

On the evening of Wednesday, July 7, 1915, there occurred on the line the most serious accident in the history of Canadian electric lines. The usual summer crowd of holidayers, including two large Sunday School picnic groups from Toronto (from Woodgreen Methodist and St. Johns Presbyterian churches) that had come over on the morning boat, dotted the park on Queenston Heights. But a sudden rainstorm at dusk sent them scurrying for the first car, and by the time the car started down the 4.2 per cent grade off the heights at 7.40 p.m. it was jammed with 154 persons, despite a normal capacity of 55. Adults, children, and picnic baskets were jammed tightly in aisles. As the car started slowly down the grade, the motorman released the sand control to stop the wheels from slipping on the wet rails. He soon discovered that the sandbox was empty. The heavy car commenced to gain speed and shot around two curves at breakneck pace, while the passengers, realizing that something was wrong, began to scream. On the third curve the car shot off the rails, down over an embankment, and turned on its side up against a tree. Fifteen persons were killed and over 100 injured. The *Chippawa* was waiting at the Queenston dock, and many of the injured were carried aboard and taken to Toronto.

The Vice-President of the International Railway Company was arrested on charges of criminal negligence, but was freed by the jury on the grounds that he could not be held responsible for neglect of duty by employees who had failed to fill the sandbox on the car. Subsequently, changes were made in the track on the grade, and various operating rules were tightened.

In 1932 when the contract expiration date approached the company notified the Parks Commission that it did not desire renewal in light of decline of business due to the automobile and the depression. Thus on September 11, 1932, operations came to an end. The commission was willing to contract with other parties, but no one was interested, and the rails were torn up. Under the terms of the original contract, the company was entitled to compensation for the value of the property. The Niagara Parks Commission offered $179,000, the salvage value, which was approved with a slight increase by an arbitration board. The International Railway appealed to the Judicial Committee of the Privy Council in London, and in a decision which, although perhaps based on a correct legal interpretation of the contract, was completely unreasonable by usual standards, the company was awarded $1 million, the reproduction cost of the property.[28] This was paid off over a period of years from hydro-electric power royalty revenue.

## NORTHERN ONTARIO

### Nipissing Central Railway Company

The most remote and isolated electric line in North America was the little Nipissing Central, incorporated by a Dominion act on April 12, 1907. The line completed five miles of track from Cobalt to Haileybury on April 30, 1910, but financial difficulties prevented further construction. On June 20, 1911, control passed from local interests to a Toronto group which sold the line to the Temiskaming and Northern Ontario (and thus to the provincial government) for $250,000. The line was extended four miles to New Liskeard in 1912 (opened November 2) and in 1914 the four-mile Cobalt–Kerr Lake branch of the T&NO (built in 1907) was turned over to the NC and electrified. Other plans for extension were never carried out. In the 1920's, however, when the T&NO built from Swastika to Noranda, Quebec, it did so under the charter and name of the NC, because its own Ontario charter did not permit the building of a line outside the province. The Noranda line was of course never electrified. In 1917, the car barn burned, destroying most of the road's equipment, which consisted primarily of four 45-foot cars and three 49-foot cars built by Preston in 1910 and 1911. The cars were replaced by three interurban cars purchased from the East St. Louis, Columbia and Waterloo in Illinois.

The road was relatively profitable prior to 1916, showing a very good return (as much as 20 per cent) on its relatively small investment. Its passenger peak was reached in 1915 (1,423,000). But the coming of the automobile and the decline of mining caused traffic to fall steadily thereafter; the 1925 total was scarcely half the peak figure, and the depression cut traffic still more. Operating deficits were incurred in 1920 and 1921, and barely avoided in the next several years. They reappeared in 1928 and continued until the road was abandoned in 1935. They were never of great magnitude, however and the road was remarkably successful in cutting expenses as traffic fell.

The light-traffic Kerr Lake branch saw the end of passenger service in 1924, and on February 9, 1935, all operations were discontinued and the tracks torn up, except for a short spur used for freight operations by the parent company. The rails of the Kerr Lake branch were removed in 1939.

## CHAPTER TEN

# QUEBEC

DESPITE THE MANY relatively densely populated areas in Quebec, only three interurban lines were ever built, as radials out of Montreal, Quebec, and Hull respectively.

*Quebec Railway, Light and Power Company*

One of the most long-lived lines was the Quebec–St. Joachim route of Quebec Railway, Light and Power Company. The line was built as a steam road, known as the Quebec, Montmorency and Charlevoix Railway Company, and electrified to Montmorency in 1900 and to St. Joachim in 1901. The same interests gained control of the Quebec street railway and the local power system, under the direction of Sir Rodolphe Forget, a Montreal financier also interested in Montreal Tramways.

The road, which for many years was operated as the Montmorency division of the Quebec Railway, with accounts separate from the city (Citadel) division until 1925, was relatively successful financially, in large measure because of the heavy travel to the famous Catholic shrine at Ste. Anne de Beaupré, near the end of the line. In addition the line offered the scenic attraction of Montmorency Falls, passing over the Montmorency River directly below the falls. The line reached Quebec City on a private right of way and paralleled the St. Lawrence once it passed the suburbs. The road was one of the earliest electric railway operators of trains of several units. The cars could not run as multiple units, but could pull several trailers. Some of the latter were original Quebec, Montmorency and Charlevoix coaches built in 1889, and used until 1959. The same interests also owned the Quebec and Saguenay, operating a steam road to Murray Bay, and using Quebec Railway tracks west of St. Joachim; the Q&S was essentially an extension of the interurban trackage. The steam road was acquired by the Grand Trunk in 1919, and thus ultimately became a part of the CNR, which continued to operate the Murray Bay trains over the interurban trackage to St. Joachim. Quebec Railway changed hands in 1922 and again in 1923, finally coming into the possession of the Shawinigan Power Company, which dominated the Quebec electric power field. On October 26, 1951, following abandonment of the street railway lines in Quebec, the interurban line was purchased outright by the CNR to ensure continued access for its Murray Bay line, and thereafter operated as part of the CNR system.

For many years there was relatively little change in operation, apart from the acquisition of six heavy steel cars in 1929, built by Ottawa Car Company, 65 feet in length, with a capacity of seventy-four passengers and weight of 85,000 pounds. As a rule about eight trains a day were operated through to St. Joachim with much more frequent service in the suburban commuting area, as far as Montmorency Falls. Traffic held up well for a number of years, but declined steadily in the fifties. In the summer of 1958 the CNR filed application for abandonment of passenger service, noting that the traffic had fallen to 1,000 passengers a day, and that the Quebec station site was desired for the new post office. Upon approval of the Board of Transport

Commissioners, service was discontinued on March 16, 1959, one week before the Port Colborne line. The track is still used for Murray Bay traffic of the CNR.

## Montreal and Southern Counties Railway Company[1]

Only one interurban was built out of Montreal, namely the Montreal and Southern Counties, the Grand Trunk's only venture into the interurban field, and the most unprofitable of all Canadian intercity electric lines. The road was incorporated by Montreal French-Canadian interests in 1897 to build from Montreal to Sherbrooke, but no actual work was done for a decade. After long negotiations, the company obtained permission to use the Victoria Bridge. Four miles, including the bridge trackage, were completed to St. Lambert, and placed in service November 1, 1909, replacing an auto bus line. For the next two years no further progress was made, except extension of track down the river to Longueil. Then, in 1911 the Grand Trunk purchased the company and commenced to extend the line in the direction of Sherbrooke. A connection was built from the original section at St. Lambert to a Central Vermont Railway line which came into Montreal from the southeast, and M&SC undertook electrification of the steam road trackage, under the supervision of Bion J. Arnold, the Chicago traction expert. Progress was now rapid; service was opened to Richelieu on June 28, 1913, to Marieville later in 1913, and to St. Césaire on May 2, 1914. From this point new track was laid to Granby, service being opened to Abbotsford on December 15, 1915, and to Granby on April 30, 1916. On January 11, 1926, the last extension (and the last on any intercity electric line in Canda) was made when the Central Vermont line from Marieville to Ste. Angèle was electrified and service established.

The main line was forty-nine miles in length, plus the four-mile Ste. Angèle branch. The road was well built, with a maximum grade of $1\frac{1}{2}$ per cent, and several substantial bridges, including one of 725 feet in length over the Richelieu River, in addition to the crossing of the St. Lawrence. Hydro-electric power from the plant at Richelieu was employed, and the road was the first DC line in Canada to use catenary construction. The Grand Trunk planned to use AC power but was persuaded against it by Arnold, partly because of the weight problem on Victoria Bridge. Central Vermont continued to operate freight service over the line until the mid-twenties and dispatching was controlled in earlier years by the CV dispatcher in St. Albans, via telephone. The M&SC acquired from the Ottawa Car Company fourteen single-end 49-foot-4-inch cars, seating fifty-six, weighing 54,500 pounds, with four Westinghouse 40-horsepower motors. The relatively small size and weight were controlled by weight limitations of the Victoria Bridge. Six 54-foot cars were ordered from the National Steel Car Company in 1915. Three 54-foot trailer cars were purchased from the Ottawa Car Company in 1917 and three 56-foot motor cars from the same firm in 1918.[2] The Windsor, Essex and Lake Shore's modern cars were purchased when that road was abandoned.

The road operated two distinct services from its station on Youville Street in lower Montreal. One was frequent suburban service, usually with single-car units, to St. Lambert, Montreal South, and Longueuil (often on twenty-minute intervals), and to Greenfield Park, Mackayville, and Brookline on the main line. Secondly, much less frequent service, at irregular intervals, was operated on the main line. Five to six trains a day went through to Granby, and a somewhat larger number terminated at Marieville; a few of the Marieville trains went on to Ste. Angèle. Multiple-unit—

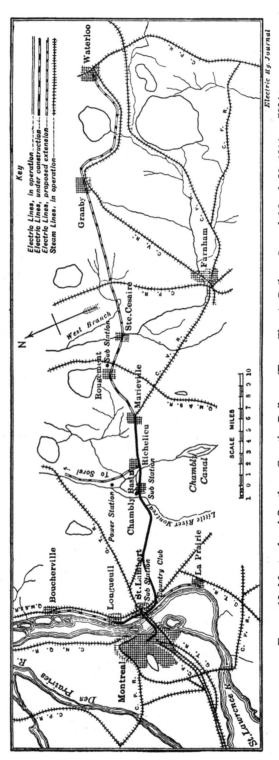

FIGURE 10. Montreal and Southern Counties Railway. (From *Electric Railway Journal*, March 28, 1914, p. 702.)

often three-unit—operation on the main line was common. The passenger traffic grew steadily, and reached a pre-depression peak of 3,435,000 in 1924; the bulk of this was, of course, suburban travel. The loss of traffic in the twenties was relatively smaller than that of any other road, and even the depression loss was not tremendous. The all-time peak of 5,732,000 passengers was reached in 1946, a figure 75 per cent greater than the previous 1924 top. Again, this was primarily suburban traffic. Despite the drop after 1946, even the 1954 figure was not much less than that for 1924. Freight traffic was never significant.

Unfortunately, however, a high and relatively stable passenger traffic did not ensure profitable operation; in the forty years from completion to 1955, in only one year did the road cover bond interest. The net earnings were substantially less after the extension was made than they had been when the road was only a suburban carrier, and operating losses were incurred in 1917, 1918, and 1920. But the continued growth of business brought a moderate profit and a rate of return of around 5 per cent up through 1930. In 1931 an operating loss appeared and continued in every one of the next twenty-four years; although, operating revenues rose over much of the period, expenses rose even faster. By 1949 the operating ratio was 142; it reached 200 in 1953 (that is, operating expenses were exactly double the operating revenues) and the phenomenal figure of 436 in the last year, 1955. In that year, operating expenses of $1,246,000 were incurred to produce $286,000 revenue. However, this represented an abnormal situation, because operations were cut off from Montreal, and cars thus were connecting with special CNR shuttle trains across Victoria Bridge. This was only a temporary arrangement.

The road had passed into the hands of the Canadian National with the parent Grand Trunk in 1920, and after the mid-twenties became a sort of neglected and forgotten stepchild. Equipment deteriorated badly, as did the track, and few changes were made in operations. Finally, in 1951 the portion of the line from Marieville to Granby was abandoned, and the latter city provided with CNR service from Central Station. The remainder of the line continued to operate amid growing deterioration until 1956 when changes to the Victoria Bridge were necessitated by the St. Lawrence Seaway, and the CNR at last acted to get rid of the serious drain on its finances and at the same time to free the space used on the bridge for urgently needed highway space. The amazing element in the history of the line is the fact that the CNR continued to operate it as long as it did at such substantial deficits; the sum of the operating deficits (after taxes) between 1931 and 1955 was $5 million. Interest over the period amounted to another $3.5 million. The deficits of the early fifties represented significant elements in the over-all net financial position of the CNR. There is some reason to believe that CNR cost allocations were such as to make the M&SC deficits appear greater than they should logically have been.

## Hull Electric Company[3]

One of the earlier intercity lines was that of the Hull Electric Company, which extended from Ottawa across the Interprovincial Bridge to Hull, Quebec, and thence to the city of Aylmer—a total of fifteen miles. The company, which from its earliest days down until 1926 was a subsidiary of the Canadian Pacific Railway, also operated the street railway system in Hull until it was abandoned in 1946.

The Ottawa terminal was under Confederation square, with platforms on either side of the CPR track leading from Union Station to the bridge; cars turned on a loop under the Chateau Laurier Hotel. The tracks extended on the roadways on each side of the CPR line across the bridge, then passed on to the streets, returned to a private right of way near the CPR station of Hull West, and ran on the CPR Waltham line right of way to the eastern edge of Aylmer. Here they again returned to the streets, running on Commercial Street to the CPR Aylmer Station. Trains with several cars were frequently used, but the equipment was not capable of multiple-unit operation. The line was placed in operation in 1897, for the most part using CPR track formerly operated by steam power.

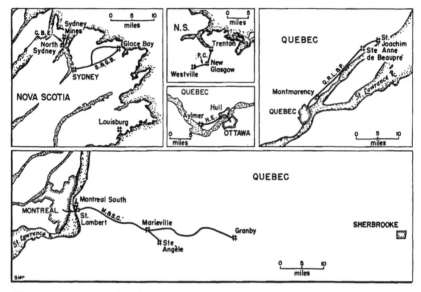

FIGURE 11. Intercity electric railway lines in Quebec and Nova Scotia. (From G. H. Hilton and J. F. Due, *The Electric Interurban Railways in America* (Stanford, 1960).)

In 1946, a fire at the Eddy Pulp plant damaged the Interprovincial Bridge, and service to Ottawa was discontinued; on April 30, 1947, the Hull-Aylmer service was also abandoned, and replaced by independent bus service. The Ottawa city system operated street car service to downtown Hull across the Chaudière Bridge until 1959.

## CHAPTER ELEVEN

# THE MARITIME PROVINCES

THE MARITIME PROVINCES had only two intercity electric lines, both in Nova Scotia, and both resembling the New England rural trolley lines more than the typical Ontario radial.

*Sydney and Glace Bay Railway Company*[1] (*Cape Breton Electric Company, Cape Breton Tramways, Limited*)

The Sydney and Glace Bay was unique in several respects: its isolated location on Cape Breton Island, the fact that it was the only Canadian line that was directly controlled by a United States holding company, and its operation for a number of years as an employee co-operative venture. The line was built as the Sydney and Glace Bay Railway, initially projected by Cape Breton Electric Company, which provided power and street railway service in Sydney. CBE was a Stone and Webster property. However, much of the land required for a right of way was owned by the Dominion Coal Company, which also operated the Sydney and Louisburg Railway, a steam road. Thus to obtain Dominion's co-operation, CBE gave it half ownership in the venture. The road was completed in 1902, with twenty-one miles of track, extending from Sydney to Glace Bay, and a loop back to Reserve Junction that gave the line the appearance of the number 6. All cars were operated counterclockwise around the loop. The area served was a thickly-settled mining and steel producing area, and cars were operated at frequent intervals and a zone fare system employed. The parent Cape Breton Electric also operated directly a six-mile interurban, completed in 1903, from its Sydney ferry connections at North Sydney to Sydney Mines. In 1911 all of the properties were merged into the CBE, the Dominion Coal accepting stock in CBE in exchange for its Sydney and Glace Bay interest.

The combination of automobile use and the depressed conditions of the area after 1931 brought the entire company into bankruptcy in 1931, and Stone and Webster permitted the company to go out of its hands. The power property was reorganized as Eastern Light and Power Company, under Nova Scotia ownership; the street railways were abandoned; and the company applied for permission to abandon the intercity line, partly because of demands of Sydney for street paving. Permission was obtained, and the company prepared to cease operations. In desperation the employees banded together and formed the Cape Breton Tramways Company Limited to take over operations. With a total investment of only about $5,000 the new company leased the property, cut wages sharply, and kept the cars in operation. The avowed purpose was merely to keep the line running for a year or so until the men could find new jobs. But the enterprise did substantially better than expected. A year later it was able to restore the old wage levels, and in 1934 to acquire several relatively new cars from the discontinued Greenfield and Montague Transportation Area line in Massachusetts. A venture designed to last a year was to operate for sixteen years. In 1946 the destruction of one of the substations by fire led to the abandonment of half of the loop line, and in 1947 the remainder was abandoned.

*Pictou County Electric Company (Egerton Tramways)*[2]

The only other intercity line in the Maritimes served the industrial area around New Glasgow in Nova Scotia. Egerton Tramways was promoted by C. Flaherty of Boston, incorporated in 1902, and commenced construction on May 21, 1904. The line started at Westville, ran along Drummond Road to Asphalt, thence on the main street of Stellarton, along the highway to the Allan mine, on a private right of way to Provost Street in New Glasgow, and on north to Trenton, a total of ten miles. A branch extended to the railway station in New Glasgow. A power house and car barn were built at Stellarton; the company generated its own power. Five 38-foot cars were initially purchased. Some service was commenced on October 11, 1904, and complete operations on April 1, 1905. The volume of traffic was of the suburban railway type, and speeds were slow.

In 1909 the company was reorganized as the Pictou County Electric Company, as an integrated power and traction enterprise. By 1924 the company was anxious to get rid of the electric railway, and the latter was acquired by the Pictou County Power Board on May 7 of that year. Operations were abandoned in May 1930 as a result of severe ice damage to the trestle across the East River at Pictou. Buses took over the service.

## CHAPTER TWELVE

# WESTERN CANADA

IN ALL WESTERN Canada there were only two intercity electric railways, one in Manitoba and one in British Columbia, but the latter was the largest single system in the Dominion.

## Winnipeg, Selkirk and Lake Winnipeg Railway Company[1]

In 1900 the Winnipeg, Selkirk and Lake Winnipeg was incorporated with the intent of building a railroad from Winnipeg to Lake Winnipeg. The road was a Mackenzie property, as was the Winnipeg Electric Company which supplied street railway and electric power service in Winnipeg. The track was laid in 1903 and 1904, and operation with steam power established from Winnipeg to Selkirk (twenty-two miles) on August 27, 1904. The decision to electrify was made in 1906, and electric service established in June 1908. In 1913 the company took over a freight spur from Middlechurch on the Selkirk line to Stony Mountain, electrified it, and in 1914 extended it to the town of Stonewall, eighteen miles from the junction. Service was inaugurated on this line on December 12, 1914. The line did not fare too badly, even though it lacked an entrance into downtown Winnipeg, trains connecting with street cars near the northern city limits.

The road developed a substantial volume of excursion traffic, using five-car trains on occasion, with a total capacity of 320. In 1913, fifty-five excursion trains were operated, for example, A number of the road's cars were built for it by the affiliated Winnipeg Electric Railway in the latter's shops, with General Electric equipment. Freight was never significant, although substantial milk traffic was handled, and ice in winter.

Passenger traffic reached its peak in 1923, with 1,196,000, double the 1915 figure, and the decline was very gradual, the 1929 figure being almost as great as that of 1923, whereas the industry as a whole lost 40 per cent of its traffic over this period. Even the depression did not cause a drastic loss, and in the last year of operation 800,000 passengers were handled. Built at a relatively late date, the line had a substantial investment per mile, and thus a rate of return that was less than typical (from 2 to 5 per cent) but remarkably stable from 1911 through 1928 (a decline in traffic in the latter year brought the figure down). However, operating deficits were avoided throughout, although in the depression years of 1932, 1934, and 1935, taxes were not covered. Of all the intercity lines which depended largely on passenger traffic, this road was the on'y one successful in more or less covering its operating expenses up to the end of the thirties. However, in part this showing was made possible only by deferring maintenance.

The best portion of the line was that to Selkirk, and in 1934 the road discontinued electric car passenger service to Stonewall. But protests over the inadequacy of the substitute bus service were so strong that the rail passenger service was resumed. On September 1, 1937, buses replaced cars on the Selkirk line, and in 1948 bus operations were sold to Beaver Bus lines, an independent operator. The railway company

H

continued to handle freight by truck until 1939, when this service was also sold to a private company. Rail passenger service, with only a few trips a day, continued from Winnipeg to Middlechurch and Stonewall until May 1, 1939 when it was replaced by an independently owned bus service.

The line was always an affiliate of the Winnipeg transit and power system, which after Mackenzie's death passed in to the hands of the Power Company of Canada

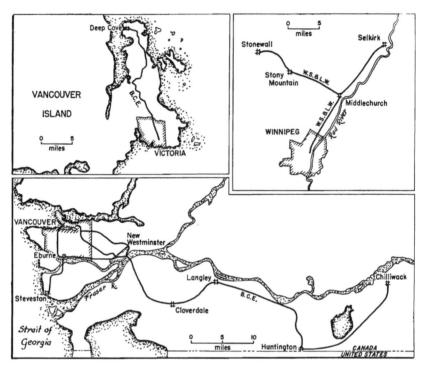

FIGURE 12. Intercity electric railway lines in western Canada. (From G. H. Hilton and J. F. Due, *The Electric Interurban Railways in America* (Stanford, 1960).)

(Nesbitt–Thomson interests). In 1931 a substantial block of stock was purchased by the Insull interests, owners of extensive power and traction systems in the United States. With the collapse of the Insull empire, control returned to Canadian hands. Eventually, the city system passed into the hands of the municipal government, and has since been operated by the Greater Winnipeg Transit Commission.

The city system for some years operated a suburban line from Winnipeg to Headingly, completed in 1913, under the name of the Suburban Rapid Transit Company.

### British Columbia Electric Railway Company[2]

The largest single intercity electric railway system in Canada, and the only one to use the familiar United States term of interurban, was that of the British Columbia Electric Railway, which had six routes and 125 miles of line. The company and its affiliates also provided urban transit service and electric power in Vancouver, Victoria, and other parts of British Columbia. The network consisted of three parts: several high-density suburban lines in the Vancouver area, a sixty-five-mile route up the Fraser Valley, built largely for freight traffic, and an isolated light-traffic line on Vancouver Island.

The first of the predecessor companies, the New Westminster and Vancouver Tramway Company Limited, built the second interurban in Canada. Extending twelve miles from Vancouver to New Westminster, it was completed in 1891. The British Columbia Electric Railway Company, incorporated in 1897, combined the street railway, power, and suburban service, and expanded rapidly in all phases of its operation. It was a British enterprise, until 1928 financed by English capital and its policies controlled from London. The guiding figure in the financial affairs of the company was Sir R. M. Horne-Payne, who was also one of Mackenzie's English associates and a director of the Canadian Northern. Mackenzie himself had no interest in BCE. The direct management of the company in the earlier years was in the hands of a Dane, Johannes E. C. Buntzen, who had emigrated to Canada many years before.

In 1905 the company leased the Vancouver and Lulu Island Railroad from the CPR and electrified it from Vancouver to Steveston for passenger service. In November, 1907 a link was completed from Eburne (called Marpole after 1917) on the Steveston line to New Westminster. Also in 1908 the company surveyed a line up the Fraser Valley, largely to handle logs, timber, and other carload freight. This road was built during 1909 and 1910, opened to Jardine on July 1, 1910, and to Chilliwack, sixty-five miles from New Westminster, in October of the latter year. A third line to New Westminster, via Burnaby Lake, was opened on June 12, 1911. Finally, on June 19, 1913, the isolated twenty-two-mile Saanich line, from Victoria to Deep Cove, was built, mainly to open a new area of Vancouver Island to settlement.[3] During this period the old lines were improved; the original Central Park line to Westminster was double tracked in 1911, and in 1912 the Highland Park cutoff was built into New Westminster to eliminate a 12 per cent grade on the streets of the town and to allow operation of two-car trains.

On the whole, track and equipment were of high standards and well maintained. Even in Vancouver the track was primarily on a private right of way, and cars reach the downtown area. The Steveston line commenced near the end of the present Granville Street Bridge, crossed on the low-level Kitislano Bridge, and ran nearly straight south, parallel to Arbutus Street and West and East boulevards to Marpole. The line crossed on its own bridge onto Lulu Island, and thence extended to Steveston on the main channel of the Fraser River. The Marpole–New Westminster line extended from a connection with the Steveston line at Marpole on a course parallel to the North Arm of the Fraser into New Westminster.

The other lines originated in the Carrall Street station, which also housed the company offices, at the eastern edge of the main business district. The Burnaby Lake line headed eastward, running close to Burnaby Lake on the south side to Sapperton and thence south to New Westminster. The main or Central Park line extended directly southeastward from its junction with the Burnaby Lake line near Commercial Drive and East 2nd Avenue to New Westminster; the Fraser line used this trackage to New Westminster, crossed the Fraser River, and swung south again, then back close to the river at Langley, east and south once more almost to the United States border at Huntington, and then northeastward into Chilliwack.

The road used a great variety of equipment, building some in its own shops and acquiring a number of Niles, Kuhlman, and American cars from the United States, as well as Preston and Ottawa cars. Multiple-unit operation was common after 1912. In early years excursion trains of open cars were pulled by electric freight motors. The New Westminster and Steveston lines used heavy steel cars in later years, often operated in pairs, and the Fraser line used high-speed wooden monitor-roof cars.

By far the most frequent service—for many years sixty trains a day each way—was provided on the Central Park line to New Westminster. Twenty trains operated to Steveston and from Eburne to New Westminster, and fifteen on the Burnaby Lake line. Typically only three trains a day were operated up the Fraser Valley. The road made very few changes in its schedules from the years before World War I until it commenced to eliminate service after 1950. The lines carried consistently about 5 million passengers a year for a long period, the population growth offsetting increased automotive use. The Central Park line to New Westminster carried half of the total, the Steveston line about 1.5 million a year, the Burnaby line 700,000, and the Fraser Valley line, in later years, only about 150,000.

During World War II traffic grew very substantially. Extensive carload freight traffic was developed and transported on long trains pulled by electric locomotives. Much of it was handled on joint rates with the steam roads, particularly the Canadian Pacific. Freight tonnage grew from 6,000 in 1902 to a high of 530,000 in 1928, fell in half in the depression, and then rose again to a new high of 1,363,000 tons in 1955, the last year of separate statistics for the electric lines.

In 1924 the company commenced bus operation to New Westminster to eliminate "jitney" competition, and co-ordinated the rail and bus service. Both bus and truck services to the Fraser Valley were inaugurated in 1926. In 1928 the Power Company of Canada (Nesbitt-Thomson) bought control of the company from the English stockholders.[4]

The system had one very weak link, the misconceived Saanich line on Vancouver Island, which was apparently built as a part of a real estate promotion scheme. The line did not serve Sidney, then the principal town on the peninsula, but bypassed it and terminated at a small settlement known as Deep Cove, where a resort hotel was built, apparently by interests affiliated with the company. The area did not develop as anticipated, and there were rarely more than six trains a day operated. On October 31, 1924, the line was abandoned, only eleven years after it was completed.[5]

The mainland system remained intact until after World War II, except for the portion of the Burnaby Lake line beyond Sapperton, abandoned July 20, 1937. The rapid growth of the area, the high quality of the service, and the extensive freight business served to avoid deficits despite the growth in automobile usage. Traffic rose greatly during World War II. After 1946, however, the company concluded that all rail passenger service, city and intercity, should be eliminated in favour of bus operation, in part because of the deteriorated condition of track and equipment. The Fraser Valley line came first, the limited passenger service being discontinued in 1949 and the line dieselized for freight service. The suburban operations were curtailed gradually. The Steveston line service was abandoned as far as Marpole on July 17, 1952, partly because the city wanted the tracks off the bridge, and the Marpole–New Westminster service on November 17, 1956. The old main line to New Westminster was abandoned beyond Park Station on October 23, 1953, and the remainder on July 15, 1954. The Burnaby Lake line was discontinued also on October 23, 1953. At the end of 1956, only the Marpole–Steveston service remained, and this was abandoned on February 28, 1958. Most of the track was retained for freight service, but the Burnaby line was completely abandoned, and the Central Park line cut back from downtown Vancouver to Nanaimo Road.

The abandonment of these private-right-of-way routes may prove to be a mistake, from the standpoint of long-run traffic congestion problems in metropolitan Vancouver.

## CHAPTER THIRTEEN

# OTHER INTERCITY OPERATIONS

A FEW OTHER lines might possibly be regarded as intercity electric lines. One was the Sudbury–Copper Cliff Suburban Electric Railway Company, its six-mile line between the two towns of its name being opened on November 11, 1915. The road was affiliated with the Mackenzie interests, and was projected in part as a freight connection for the Canadian Northern to Copper Cliff. This plan did not materialize when the Canadian Northern passed into Dominion hands in 1917, and the line was used primarily to transport miners to and from work. The original car came from Toronto and York Radial; when the Schuykill Railway was abandoned in the thirties some of its cars came to the Sudbury line, and Wilkes Barre Railway equipment was acquired during World War II. The line was abandoned in 1950.

The Mount McKay and Kakabeka Falls line was projected from Fort William to the Falls, but never got farther than five miles out of town. It used steam except on city streets, and its chief business was freight switching and the hauling of gravel.

The Levis County Tramways in the province of Quebec was in part an intercity trolley line, using street railway equipment but operating from Levis to St. Romuald and other adjacent towns. It was built in 1903. A fire in 1921 destroyed almost all of its cars, but it eventually resumed service on April 12, 1922, and electric service operated until 1946.

The Berlin and Bridgeport operated five miles of line from Kitchener to Bridgeport, and was projected to Guelph. In 1923 it was taken over by the city of Kitchener and operated as a part of the city system until its abandonment in 1939.

The Oshawa Railway was (and is) a very important freight hauler, connecting the General Motors plants and other factories with the CNR, into whose hands it passed with its parent Grand Trunk in 1920. So far as passenger service was concerned, it was essentially a street car line, but showed its service in the *Official Guide to the Railways* as though it were an intercity railroad, operating from Ross Corners via Oshawa to Lake, 4.4. miles. Buses were substituted for electric cars on January 28, 1940, but freight service was operated with electricity until dieselization in 1964. The bus service was turned over to other operators in 1959.

The Britannia line of the Ottawa city system was opened in 1900 and operated until 1959. Originally it ran through rural country on a private right of way. A twelve-mile side-of-the-road line using city cars operated from Edmonton to St. Albert, Alberta.

There were two electric lines that were primarily freight haulers. One was the Shawiningan Falls Terminal Company in Quebec, the other the Western Power Company of Canada line from Ruskin to Austins, B.C. (six miles).

## LINES PARTIALLY CONSTRUCTED BUT NEVER OPERATED

In part I, reference was made to the large number of projected lines for which charters were obtained, but which were never built. On a few of these construction was actually undertaken, although never completed.

## Ontario West Shore

Originally chartered in 1902 as the Ontario, Bruce and Grey, the West Shore was projected from Goderich to Kincardine, paralleling the shore of Lake Huron. The local promoters enlisted the aid of one J. W. Moyes, a Toronto transit "expert" who apparently had had some connection with the Metropolitan (Toronto and York Radial). In 1908, Goderich, Kincardine, and the intermediate townships guaranteed $385,000 of bonds to build the line. The road was graded between the two towns, and, between 1908 and 1911, sixteen miles of track laid from Goderich to Kintail by the Huron Construction Company, owned by Moyes.

In 1911 all of the funds from the bonds were exhausted, and an investigation for the cities by an engineer of the Ontario Railway and Municipal Board found that only $228,000 had been spent, and that $175,000 had disappeared. Moyes at first claimed that he could not finish the project because Ontario Hydro had blocked his plans for a power dam on the Maitland River. He refused to co-operate with the official investigation, claiming that he could not remember details of the finances and that he had turned the records over to another man who had since died. This statement was found to be false, and records in a trunk discovered by Toronto police indicated irregularities. Moyes refused to attend hearings on the grounds of illness, and when a warrant was finally issued for his arrest he took a train for Algonquin Park where he was last seen at Scotia Junction; never again was a trace found of him, so far as is known. The investigation disclosed a serious misuse of funds, and the engineer in charge certified that work had been done in excess of the actual amounts paid.

The towns negotiated unsuccessfully with the CPR and independent interests to take over the line, and finally sold the rails to Ontario Hydro for use on the Chippawa project construction line. About $100,000 was thus salvaged, the municipalities being saddled with the remaining $285,000. The line never operated. One of the ironies in the whole picture was the fact that in the midst of the investigation, Moyes was hired by the Toronto Railway Company for advice!

## Toronto Eastern Railway

The Toronto Eastern was equally ill fated, although no fraud was involved. After the early plans to extend the Toronto and Scarborough to Oshawa had failed, in 1911 a group of Oshawa business men, including Robert McLaughlin, the famous car manufacturer, incorporated the Toronto Eastern to build a high-speed line between the two cities. It was soon taken over by the ubiquitous Mackenzie, who promised to build it from Toronto to Cobourg in order to soothe the feelings of Oshawa and nearby towns over the locating of the Canadian Northern lakeshore line several miles to the north (for topographical reasons). Grading was started in 1912, and by 1913 fifteen miles of track had been laid from Bowmanville to Whitby, and grading was continued to Pickering. But the development of plans for a Hydro radial line east from Toronto caused the TE to cease construction; the war intervened, and the line passed to the Dominion government with its parent company.

After the Hydro plans fell through, the CNR became interested in building the line itself; in 1923, substantial reconstruction of the previously built portion was undertaken, and additional work carried out. New ties were laid and bridges rebuilt. Four more miles of track were laid on the section between Whitby and Pickering. Suddenly, in 1924 construction was stopped. The government was evasive about its plans for a while, but by 1925 announced that it had abandoned the whole project in light of increased automobile use. The rails were then torn up without ever having been used. The route of most of the line followed highway 2. Various alternative plans were developed for the entrance into Toronto, but, of course, were never carried out.

### Dunnville, Wellandport and Beamsville Electric Railway

This line was projected from Dunnville to a connection with the Hamilton, Grimsby and Beamsville at Beamsville. Most of the grading between the two towns was finished in 1909, but before rails were laid the promoters ran out of funds. An attempt was made to resume construction in 1914, but nothing more was ever accomplished.

# NOTES

## CHAPTER ONE

1. This description is based on contemporary newspaper accounts. See also Upper Canada Railway Society, *Newsletter*, April 1961, p. 6.
2. *Street Railway Journal*, vol. IX (July 1893), p. 446.

## CHAPTER TWO

1. See *Canadian Railway and Marine World*, June 1916, p. 240.

## CHAPTER FOUR

1. See *Canadian Railway and Marine World*, May 1925, p. 248.

## CHAPTER FIVE

1. See *Reports of Commission Appointed to Inquire into Hydro-Electric Railways* (Toronto, 1921).

## CHAPTER NINE

1. See *Canadian Railway and Marine World*, June 1913, pp. 281–84, for a contemporary description.
2. See *Electric Railway Journal*, vol. XI (Oct. 1925), pp. 37–38.
3. See *Canadian Railway and Marine World*, Oct. 1923, pp. 489–90.
4. *Ibid.*, Jan. 1918, p. 37, for a review of the legal issues.
5. *Ibid.*, Dec. 1928, p. 737.
6. See *Electric Railway Journal*, vol. XXXIII (Jan. 2, 1909), pp. 8–10.
7. These were in Appleton, Wisconsin; Baltimore; Detroit; Montgomery, Alabama, by far the largest installation; Scranton; Port Huron; and Denver (all 1886 except Baltimore, 1885).
8. See *Canadian Railway and Marine World*, Oct. 1934, p. 444.
9. See *Street Railway Journal*, vol. XXXI (Jan. 11, 1908), pp. 38–42; and *Eledtric Railway Journal*, vol. XL (Nov. 30, 1912), pp. 1096–98.
10. See *Canadian Railway and Marine World*, Aug. 1928, p. 494, and Oct. 1929, p. 644.
11. *Ibid.*, Oct. 1913, p. 493.
12. *See Ibid.*, July 1927, p. 425, and Aug. 1927, p. 485.
13. *Ibid.*, Oct. 1912, p. 518.
14. *See ibid.*, July 1915, pp. 266–70; and Terry T. M. Ferris, "History of the London and Port Stanley Railway 1852–1946," (unpublished M.A. thesis, University of Western Ontario Library).
15. Most of the remainder of the stock had been sold by the municipalities to individuals, and eventually was acquired by the Grand Trunk, and thus passed to the CNR.
16. See *Street Railway Journal*, vol. XI (Jan. 1895), pp. 49–52.
17. See *Canadian Railway and Marine World*, Feb. 1916; and *Electric Railway Journal*, vol. XLVII (March 18, 1916), pp. 986–88.
18. See *Electric Railway Review*, vol. XXIX (Feb. 8, 1908), pp. 177–78; and *Woods* v. *Grand Valley Ry. Co.*, 27 OLR 556, 1912.
19. Abandonment was recommended as early as 1925 by a consulting engineering firm. See *Canadian Railway and Marine World*, Dec. 1925, p. 625.
20. *Ibid.*, Oct. 1927, p. 608.
21. See L. H. Pursley, *Street Railways of Toronto* (Los Angeles, Interurbans Special no. 25, 1958).

22. See *Railway and Marine World*, July 1911, pp. 677–78; *Canadian Railway and Marine World*, March 1916, pp. 110–17, 196; May 1917, pp. 197–98; and Aug. 1917, pp. 320–22.

23. *Canadian Railway and Marine World*, Dec. 1924, p. 626.

24. See *Railway and Marine World*, July 1908, pp. 513–14; *Canadian Railway and Marine World*, July, 1913, pp. 339–42; *Street Railway Journal*, vol. XVIII (Feb. 15, 1901), p. 173, and (Sept. 7, 1901), pp. 284–86.

25. See *Canadian Railway and Marine World*, Jan. 1924, p. 33, and Dec. 1924, p. 625.

26. *Ibid.*, Feb. 1931, p. 108; *Merritton v. Niagara, St. Catharines and Toronto Ry. Co.*, 38 CRC 227, 1931.

27. See *Street Railway Journal*, vol. XI (Oct. 1895), pp. 41–44; vol. XIII (Oct. 1897), pp. 593–97.

28. *International Railway Co. v. Niagara Parks Commission*, 45 CRC 142, 1935; 46 CRC 257, 1937.


## CHAPTER TEN

1. See *Electric Railway Journal*, vol. XLIII (March 28, 1913), pp. 702–04. See also *Canadian Railway and Marine World*, Sept. 1913, pp. 436–40, and Aug. 1916, pp. 332–33.

2. See *Canadian Railway and Marine World*, March 1918, p. 114.

3. The author is indebted to the Canadian Pacific Railway Co. for virtually all the information on Hull Electric. See also *Canadian Railway and Marine World*, Sept. 1913, p. 441.


## CHAPTER ELEVEN

1. See *Railway and Marine World*, April 1911, p. 359.

2. See *Railway and Shipping World*, Nov. 1904, p. 406.


## CHAPTER TWELVE

1. See *Canadian Railway and Marine World*, Jan. 1913, p. 37.

2. See *Electric Railway Journal*, vol. XXIV (Oct. 2, 1909), pp. 529–32; *Street Railway Review*, vol. XIV (July 20, 1904), pp. 461–64; *Railway and Marine World*, Nov. 1908, pp. 844–46, and Jan. 1911, pp 67–71.

3. See *Canadian Railway and Marine World*, May 1913, p. 233.

4. See *ibid.*, June 1928, p. 354.

5. See *Electric Railway Journal*, vol. LXII (Sept. 1923), p. 445, and vol. LXIII (Dec. 1924), p. 628.

# MAJOR REFERENCES

## PERIODICALS

*Canadian Railway and Marine World*, designated as *Railway and Shipping World* from 1898 to 1904; *Railway and Marine World*, 1905–1912 (July); *Canadian Railway and Marine World*, 1912 (Aug.)–1936; *Canadian Transportation* from 1937 to the present. This publication, the trade journal of the transportation industry in Canada, is an invaluable reference source on the electric lines from their earliest years down to the present. For many years the issues contained a separate section on electric railways.

*Electric Railway Journal*, formed in 1908 as a consolidation of the *Street Railway Journal* (founded 1884), and the *Electric Railway Review* (founded 1891 as the *Street Railway Review* and operated under that name until 1906); became the *Transit Journal* in 1932, and discontinued 1942. This was the principal trade journal in the field in the United States, and contained substantial reference to Canadian developments.

Upper Canada Railway Society, *Newsletter* and *Bulletin* (Toronto, 1941–present). Several of the bulletins have been devoted to electric lines, and the newsletters have frequently contained references to current developments.

Canadian Railroad Historical Association, *Bulletin* (Montreal, 1931–present). Various bulletins deal with electric railways.

## STATISTICS AND STATUTORY HISTORIES

Canada, Deputy Minister of Railways and Canals, *Railway Statistics of the Dominion of Canada* (Ottawa, annually, 1893–1918). These reports included electric railways as well as steam railways, with a separate section for electric railways from 1901. In 1919 responsibility for railway statistics was transferred to DBS.

Canada, Dominion Bureau of Statistics, *Statistics of Railways in Canada* (Ottawa, annually, 1919–22); *Statistics of Electric Railways of Canada* (Ottawa, annually, 1922–55). This is a continuation of the series (noted above) compiled by the office of the Deputy Minister of Railways and Canals, although after 1921 the electric railway statistics were published as a separate report. The series provides detailed statistics of the individual lines, year by year, together with information on new lines and abandonments.

Canada, Department of Transport, *A Statutory History of Steam and Electric Railways of Canada, 1836–1937* (Ottawa, 1938). This volume contains brief summaries of the incorporating acts for all steam and electric lines. An appendix was published in 1954.

## BOOKS, REPORTS, AND MONOGRAPHS

Due, J. F., *Sir Adam Beck and the Hydro Radial Proposals* (Toronto, Upper Canada Railway Society Bulletin no. 50 (1958). A detailed review of the radial plans.

Hilton, G. H., and J. F. Due, *The Electric Interurban Railways in America* (Stanford, 1960). The history of the United States interurbans, with some reference to Canada.

Pursley, L. H., *Street Railways of Toronto* (Los Angeles, Interurbans Special no. 25, 1958). A detailed history of the Toronto railways up to the time of municipal operation.

*Reports of Commission Appointed to Inquire into Hydro-Electric Railways* (Toronto, 1921). The Sutherland Commission report on the radial proposals, together with considerable discussion of existing electric lines.

# INDEX

Numbers in italics after the name of a railway company refer to the section which outlines the history of that company.

Lightning Source UK Ltd.
Milton Keynes UK
UKHW030613210722
406167UK00006B/665

9 781442 631335